Rest

YOUR PLACE OF VICTORY

GINGER LEVI

Copyright © 2016 by Ginger Levi

Rest
Your Place of Victory
by Ginger Levi

Printed in the United States of America.
Edited by Xulon Press.

ISBN 9781498485746

All rights reserved solely by the author. The author guarantees all contents are original and do not infringe upon the legal rights of any other person or work. No part of this book may be reproduced in any form without the permission of the author. The views expressed in this book are not necessarily those of the publisher.

Unless otherwise indicated, Scripture quotations taken from the King James Version (KJV) – public domain

www.xulonpress.com

Table of Contents

Acknowledgments vii
Endorsements ix
Foreword xiii
Introduction xvii
Chapter One—Putting Out Fires 23
Chapter Two—Running On Empty 32
Chapter Three—Invitation 48
Chapter Four—Yield 66
Chapter Five—A New Perspective 86
Chapter Six—Hiding Place 101
Chapter Seven—Active Waiting 120
Chapter Eight—Restoration 144
Chapter Nine—Remain 161
Chapter Ten—Abide 185
Appendix 207
References 209

Acknowledgments

First of all, I want to give thanks and praise to my Lord and Savior Jesus Christ, without whom I would not have been able to write this book. I am so thankful for the Holy Spirit's guidance and revelation during this process. No growth process is ever easy, but I'm so thankful for God's grace and mercy, as well as His patience.

Next, I want to thank my wonderful husband Dan, who was the first to point out to me that I am a "bad rester." His love and support over the last 22 years have been a gift from God to my life. Thank you also to my three children, Brianna, Ryan, and Eric. I love you all so very much!

My deepest thanks to my team of "helpers"—you guys are the best! Lorna, you have been one of my closest friends since the age of six. I so appreciate your mad skills at editing and your unending patience with my lack of technological skills. Nell, my lunchtime buddy and one of the sweetest, yet most persistent people I know, thank you for consistently asking "So, how's the book coming?" I kept writing so that

I wouldn't disappoint you! You are a terrific cheerleader! Tazmin, thank you for your encouragement and "deadlines"—they worked! I even came in two weeks under deadline! Karen, you are my sister in faith and fellow lover of books! You always encourage me! Kim, my sister, you have loved me through thick and thin, good and bad, high and low—I so appreciate the support over the last ten years—you are the best! Pam, thank you for your prayer and support for the last twelve years. You'll never know how much you mean to me! Pastor Scott Pyle—God is so gracious to bring us together again after thirty years!

Finally, to my pastors, Jayson and Cori Heath, thank you for loving our family and supporting us in all that God has called us to do. You are awesome examples of the love of Christ in action and we are thankful to be a part of Alexandria First Assembly!

Endorsements

Exactly what every person needs to read! The scriptures that are coupled with the life giving truths in this book will set you free.

Jayson and Cori Heath
Alexandria First Assembly of God, Alexandria, Louisiana

Rest: personally I'm all for it! In the business of day-to-day life, at the end of the day, I want to come home, get clean, eat and *rest!* Theoretically that's my goal, but in practicality, it rarely happens. People have told me for years, "You need to learn to rest." For all intents and purposes that is true, naturally and spiritually. Man's idea of rest will result in an empty tank at some mile marker along life's highway every time. God's plan for rest however, will bring you to His ultimate desire for us all; abundant life, walking in His righteousness, freedom from fear and feasting on His goodness as our cup runneth over!

What I have enjoyed so much about this book is how Ginger exposes the plan the enemy has to keep us from God's rest, and then she takes us on a journey throughout the Holy Word of God piecing together His plan for us to enter His rest! Through His word she puts together, like a puzzle, the precise, in depth plan it is, yet so easy to achieve.

As I read I felt like I was receiving encouragement from a coach at half time. Ginger spurs the reader on with inspiring thought and God's truth. She made this sometimes over complicated purpose of God, not only easy to understand, but she also infuses your spirit with an *I can do this* determination.

Rest—Your Place of Victory is a must-read and you will re-read it over and over again, until *rest* becomes your *absolute victory!*

Scott Pyle
Shift Ministry

I have been blessed to have Ginger as my friend so long that I don't remember not having her in my life. It's fair to say we helped raise each other from the roots up. So when I read the first sentence of this book, I laughed because it speaks a lifelong truth for both of us. She and I are both "bad resters" and it's probably one of the reasons we became such close friends. We were driven from a young age to be the best we could be and our efforts were rewarded with high achievement and success. But they came with great personal cost.

For much of my life, I carried a deep fear that if I stopped and rested for even just a moment, the truth would be revealed and I would be exposed as a fraud and a failure. So I worked endlessly and lived with a spirit crushing level of stress and anxiety every single day. Then, over 20 years ago, I was saved. I accepted Christ as my savior and was immensely relieved to learn that He would carry my burdens and I could give Him all my fear, anxiety and perfectionism. Over the years, in my talks with God, I have often said, "God, I'm giving you my worries and my problems. Thank you for taking them." But, the truth is, I didn't really give them *all* to Him. I said I did, but I didn't. I kept a lot for myself. And, worse, I kept myself from Him through my inability to truly rest. Often when I was with Him, I was really somewhere else. And of course, He knew it. So, when Ginger asked me to help edit her book, God did what God does and used this opportunity to speak directly to my heart. I was convicted from that first sentence and with each word I read and each example she provided, I found myself shaking my head and thanking God for the gift of this book and the gift of her friendship. Ginger will show you how and why building a relationship with God by entering into His rest is vital. Resting in Him is the key to the door that leads to *everything.* Read this book, unlock that door and claim your victory!

Lorna M. Eby
Former book editor and lifelong friend

Foreword

Shortly after being asked to write the foreword for this work I had the opportunity to practice what I learned while reading the manuscript. My daughter, pregnant with her first child, called to say her water had broken at 2:00 A.M. and they were en route to the hospital. The requisite middle-of-the-night phone calls were made to loved ones. Within the hour we sat huddled together in the waiting room eagerly anticipating news of our baby girl's arrival. Instead, an uncomfortable period passed in which the frequent, "newsy" texts from the proud father, who was standing watch during delivery, came to an end. From where I sat at a small table under a window, I bowed my head and tried to pray, but the words would not come. My mind was a tangle of thoughts vying for attention and analysis. Why had he stopped texting? Why was he not responding to texts from his mother or me? Would anyone else be giving us an update? Was something wrong?

Anxious chatter and meaningless small talk swirled among the assembly. I strained to pray and distance my mind from the surroundings. As I closed my eyes, I chose to set my affection on Him. As if emerging from a thick fog, the face of Jesus came into view. The trace of a smile was on His lips, and I could feel my heart relax. The apprehension attempting to overwhelm my peace lifted off me. In that moment, my heart knew that all was well.

We would later learn that challenges during the birth resulted in serious respiratory issues for my newborn granddaughter. Immediately following her birth, she was whisked into the nursery for further assessment. It would be three long days before her parents would hold her for the first time. Nevertheless, her little body flourished while on oxygen and a constant drip of nutrients and medication. She made significant improvements by the hour. We sighed relief at the news that she would be unfazed by her traumatic entry into this world, thinking the remainder of the hospital stay would be unremarkable.

However, on the morning after giving birth, my daughter awoke to strange symptoms culminating in a heart rate of 250 beats per minute for more than 15 minutes during a sudden onset of postpartum tachycardia. Only one such episode took place, but the memory of its duration and intensity generated anxiety attacks in my daughter for the next three days. It was during this series of events—a routine birthing experience gone haywire and a frightening cardiac event in my otherwise healthy 22 year old daughter—that gave me a new appreciation for the gift of being permitted to enter the rest of God.

Ginger Levi explains the rest of God in a conversant, relatable manner. She discusses the rest of God neither as a mere religious practice nor as a crisis-mandated exercise, but as a permanent spiritual destination for accessing strong faith to succeed in everyday life. In this work, she offers a practical guide to help enter God's rest and dwell in a spiritual atmosphere thoroughly infused with His power and presence. While the pressures of this life assail everyone, those who recognize and understand the profound power of entering God's rest will find the strength necessary to stand. Truly, the rest of God is a warfare strategy of great significance for the hour in which we live.

Karen Satterfield
Speaker and Ministry Consultant

Introduction

My whole life I've been what my husband refers to as a bad "rester." I'm not sure if it's because of the way I was raised, where I was raised (I'm a Yankee), or if it's genetics. All the same, it's true—I'm bad at resting. I've always felt a strange sense of guilt at being what my grandmother referred to as "idle." I jokingly tell people that I have only two speeds—full speed and off! Unfortunately, it is hard to maintain this in real life, especially over long periods of time. I've always told myself to "keep moving" and get it all done (whatever "all" is) before I allow myself to sit down.

Unfortunately, having this mindset usually leads to feelings of frustration. It is almost like a full-fledged battle raging inside of me. Part of me (the "good, responsible" one) pressures me to keep going, to fulfill any "duty" whether actual or self-imposed. The magnitude of the task or project doesn't seem to matter, just the feeling that I "should." On the other side of the ring is the "rebellious" part, the one that wants to chuck it all and goof off. This part rarely wins out, and when it does, I experience an almost immediate sense of guilt. There has to be a happy medium somewhere between these polar opposites, but I have never been good at finding it. I feel frustrated with myself because I can't rest and frustrated with others who don't seem to have the same problem I do. I've told myself for years that others who don't share my inability to slow down are lazy or unmotivated; but the truth is, I long to be like them. I want to be able to enjoy life and I want to live excellently. But what does that mean? Is excellence only tied to productivity and making sure that all the things that need to get done get done? For me, the answer for many years has been yes, but now I'm certain that true excellence in life is achieved by *balance,* and not the balance that I can dream up, but rather the balance that comes from a life dictated by God's agenda and not my own. Counter-intuitive, I know, but altogether true.

So, the "million-dollar question" is how did I get there from here? And how can you do the same? If it were something that I could have done on my own I would have done it by long before now! Most of us do not want to stay in a state where we feel caught up in every wind of drama, continually frustrated and exhausted, but with little to show for it. I can't count the times that I cried my eyes out to God, asking for answers to messes I had gotten myself into, seeking Him to somehow wave a magic wand and make everything better. While He indeed can (and will) make things better, we must learn to work with Him, to do things according to His plan

Introduction

and on His terms. Just as there are rules for driving, credit, school and work, there are rules for entering into His rest.

This is how He finally got my attention. God used my propensity for being a rule-abider against me. He asked me one day about a year ago if I was ready to trade my stress for His rest. During this time, frankly, I was worn out. We had had two children graduate from high school and leave home, only to go through trials. We had to bring one home (with a sense of irritation, I might add) and the other was struggling to make it on her own in an apartment that we deemed unsafe, with a companion we were less than happy about. In my motherly role, I wanted to do all that I could to assist them financially, practically and spiritually. We took on financial challenges and were stretched to the limits of our patience. We found ourselves extremely crowded with the addition of another household's furniture, clothing, books and other stuff.

So, when God asked me the question, I admit that I was a bit offended. I mean, couldn't God see that I had enough going on and that I was at the end of my rope? I sensed that He was serious, however, and realized that this might be my only opportunity to learn how to truly enter into His rest, so despite my upset, I answered "yes, Lord." It was then that God began to patiently instruct me on the subject of rest, which was more detailed and dynamic than I ever imagined. He began by telling me that I needed to learn to trust Him. Again, a bit of frustration surfaced! After all, I had been saved for about twenty-eight years by this time, and for twenty-three of those years I had been filled with the Holy Spirit! Instead of acting on my frustration, however, I asked Him what He meant. He guided me to look up the definition of the word "trust" to ensure that I understood it fully. I have always loved words, so I have two different dictionary apps on my phone. What I found in the definition forever changed my perspective.

The definition of trust, at its core, is the belief that someone or something is reliable, good, honest, and effective. It also includes having an assured reliance on the character, ability, strength or truth about someone or something. In order to have real trust, we must get to know someone and see him or her "in action," so to speak. I thought about the definition and felt an inner conviction that perhaps, despite having served the Lord for almost three decades, I may not have actually put my complete trust in Him. I wondered if somehow, deep down, I expected Him to be not much different than the people I encountered in life. That while He is good, maybe I didn't qualify for the full outpouring of His goodness, leading me to be cautiously optimistic, at best, of the results I could expect in my life.

John 15:13 tells us that there is no greater display of love than to lay down one's life for a friend. This kind of love is exactly the kind that God has for us! Through His Son, Jesus Christ, He yielded up His own life. Jesus' will and desires were wrapped up in doing what God called Him to do in order to reconcile us to the Father. The ultimate sacrifice on the cross is proof not only of His love for us but of His character. He set aside what His flesh and mind would have chosen to follow God's plan. He is completely trustworthy! I had known this and confessed it, but now it seemed like the lights were turned on and I could see clearly. No longer did I have to doubt His trustworthiness, for He was not like any other I had ever met. It was on the heels of this revelation that God showed me that even as Jesus laid down His life in obedience to the will of the Father, I, too, must do so if I wanted to experience His rest.

Galatians 2:20 calls us to be crucified with Christ (extinguishing and subduing our passions and selfishness) so that the life we are living in the here and now can be hidden in Him. We can exchange our stress for His rest by allowing our lives to be yielded up to His purpose and plan. This is the posture of rest.

Chapter 1

Putting Out Fires

Satan is a master at distraction. He delights in seeing us running back and forth trying to put out the fires, big and small, that he sets in our lives. He knows that if he can keep us occupied with distractions, we will remain in a state of upset and be unable to enter God's rest, which is our place of victory. This tactic is one that is quite effective in the lives of most people, including many believers. For me, I felt like I had spent a lifetime running from one crisis to another, trying vainly to get things "under control." Little did I understand that they were under control, but unfortunately, it was the wrong control.

Our adversary is sneaky! He wants us to buy into the idea that chaos and frenzy is just a part of "living in the world today" and to resign ourselves to it, accepting it as a way of life. It's easy to get caught up and distracted by all the details of life, to end up living day-to-day or minute-to-minute, acutely away of the next "thing" that must get done. God showed me that it takes a conscious decision to step out of the frenetic mode and rest. The world doesn't make it easy. There is always a high demand for our attention from phones, emails, social media, and 24-hour news updates. But this tactic is not a new one for Satan. He's been busy for thousands of years starting fires and leading the distracted away from the path that the Lord has for them. By keeping us distracted, he is able to keep us from focusing our attention on the only One who is truly worthy. When this happens we forfeit what is rightfully ours, His peace. When we keep our eyes on Him, the stress and anxiety fade away, eclipsed by His glory and peace. I love the words to the song *Turn Your Eyes Upon Jesus:*

"Turn your eyes upon Jesus, look full in His wonderful face, and the things of earth will grow strangely dim in the light of His glory and grace."

That is our promise! When our souls are quiet we can hear His voice telling us which details are important. Luke 22:7–13 gives the account of Jesus instructing His disciples and giving explicit directions, down to the most minute details. Verse 13 records that "they went and found it just as He had said to them." We can't afford to live a life so noisy and cluttered that we can't hear what He is saying to us, for this is how we remain on the proper path.

Patience is not something we have much practice with in modern society. We have come to depend on microwaves,

Instagram, and drive-throughs as a way of life. Five minutes is too long to wait to be served our fast food. And while these conveniences have their benefits, we have become an irritable, angry bunch who can't wait or delay gratification for much. Psalms 37 instructs us to rest in the Lord and wait patiently in the Lord, not fretting (becoming angry, jealous, displeased, or grieved) because of what others are doing (Ps. 37:7). The concept of rest, standing still and quieting myself, was something that was foreign but so desperately needed. God was indeed showing me this powerful truth, as if for the first time. Instead of fretting, we are to trust Him, believing that He will bring our successful pathway/journey to pass (Ps. 37:5). This is the opposite of becoming agitated, impatient and complaining about things "taking too long." It requires us to believe not only in Him, but also in His ability to bring what we need to pass at just the right time! In other words, we must take Proverbs 3:5–6 to heart and trust in the Lord with all our hearts, leaning not to our own understanding or way of doing things. It's true that His ways aren't our ways (Isa. 55:8)—they are so much better! God's timing is always perfect. When we trade our impatience for trust in Him, our agenda for His proper path, we are able to exchange our stress for His rest.

We all know that day-to-day life can be messy. It's possible to get tangled up in stress, strife, and bad attitudes or sticky situations quite inadvertently. What are we to do when we find ourselves where we wish we weren't and how can we keep this from happening in the future? The answer is simple; we need to be *kept.* 1 Peter 1:5 tells us that as Disciples of Christ we are "kept by the power (ability, strength, might and miracle) of God through faith." Now that's good news! A similar Old Testament reference is found in Isaiah 26:3 where it states that God will keep us in perfect peace when our minds are stayed (focused) on Him because we trust Him. My favorite scripture reference about being kept is found in Philippians 4:7 where it states that the peace (prosperity, quietness, rest and wholeness) of God which passes all understanding (intellect, mind, thoughts, feelings) shall keep (protect) our hearts and minds through Christ Jesus. When we are seeking after God, looking to Him and focusing on Him, taking the time to both talk and listen, He promises to set up guards as sentinels for us. How? Through His peace—the rest and quiet assurance we have knowing Who He is and what He has done (and is doing) for us through Christ. Now when we notice we are becoming entangled or getting off course, we simply have to get right back to His peace—the secret place where we find rest and strength. And, as we do, He faithfully teaches and trains us to remain under the protection that His peace affords, helping us to truly abide in this place.

Think of it as being like a home improvement project. Anyone who has done any type of home improvement project has found out that unless you carefully measure, it is easy to be "off." It's very disconcerting to spend time and energy working on a project only to discover in the end that your results don't "line up" the way they should. No matter how pretty the picture you've used, if you neglect to measure or "match up" your project to this reference throughout the process, in the end it will fail to be an accurate reflection of your intention. I've discovered that Christian life is much like this. Although we may start out on track, if we fail to continually check our measurements by immersing ourselves in His Word and spending time in prayer and instruction, it is easy to miss the mark. Proverbs 11:1 declares that dishonest scales are an abomination to the Lord. When we fail to use His unchanging truth as our rule and compass, lining our words and ways up with His plumb line, it is actually idolatry! This simply means we are putting something, typically ourselves (e.g. our way, opinion, intellect, comfort) above His wisdom and guidance. Proverbs 11:1 goes on to say that just weights are His delight. It seems that when we spend time dwelling with Him and learning His ways and His Word, the building process not only goes well, but it is acceptable and a pleasure. In other words, the building Inspector approves of the design and execution. It is in this type of building that His favor is found and costly mistakes are avoided. Any good contractor will tell you that the savings in time, money and aggravation, as well as reputation, far outweigh any advantage of failing to follow the guidelines for construction. Abiding with the Master Builder means having access to the blueprint for success.

Luke 10 is a familiar passage of scripture that illustrates how stress looks. At the end of this chapter, we find Mary and Martha, the sisters of Lazarus, in the company of Jesus. I admit that at times I've felt righteously indignant on Martha's behalf; after all, she had to do all the work of entertaining Jesus and the disciples (cooking, cleaning, serving) while her sister sat down at Jesus' feet and listened to His sermon. It seems unfair, doesn't it? In truth, Jesus pointed out Martha's true issue—she was distracted, anxious, and full of cares about all kinds of things. I've been there more times than I want to admit! Imagine getting ready for a big celebration such as a party to honor a loved one or major life event. There are all the details to juggle—invitations, venue, decorations, and menu. Depending on the event and your personality, delegation of details may seem impossible, yet more than anything, you desire (and require) help to get everything done within the time allotted. Stress mounts as the deadline draws near; the joyous event suddenly becomes a source of burden, even panic. When all you can see is the mountain of tasks and issues looming before you, you begin to feel overwhelmed and alone. This is a trap that Satan sets to not only keep you from spending time with God, but to make you angry and offended with the body of Christ and alienate you from those who are put in your life to love and disciple you in the faith. In Luke 10:42, Jesus plainly states that there is *one* thing that is needed, one primary necessity in our lives, and that is spending time in His presence. It is when we purposefully set aside our mountain of "must-dos" and read His Word, spending time praying and worshiping Him, that He can minister strength, wisdom, peace and ability to us. When you believe you don't have the time to do this, remember that it's unlikely that we could actually complete our "must-dos" in that time anyway. This is the reason that Jesus said that spending time with Him is the primary necessity—it benefits everything else in our lives and equips us to perform everything we set our hands to.

Paul, who wrote two-thirds of the New Testament, knew as well as anyone that pressures could pile up and feel like a crushing weight. He knew that assignments from the enemy were stacked up against him and he even asked God repeatedly to remove them, after all, Paul was a missionary, doing the work of the Lord. It was then that God revealed His secret to overcoming feeling pressured and overwhelmed—resting in Him. In 2 Corinthians 12:9, God tells Paul that His grace (benefit, favor, joy, thanksgiving, gift) is sufficient for Paul. The scripture goes on to say that God's strength is made perfect in Paul's weakness. The Greek word translated as "strength" is the word *dunamis.* Often, when words from the Greek or Hebrew language are translated into English, they lose some of their "punch." According to the Strong's Concordance, the full meaning of the word includes miraculous power, ability, might and abundance. The word perfect encompasses the idea that things are finished, accomplished, and full. In other words, in the midst of trouble, chaos, stress and upset, we can rest in Him, trusting that His miraculous power will be enough for every situation, bringing about all the ability that is needed to accomplish His will through us! In fact, our God specializes in victories when the odds appear impossible!

Resting in the midst of tests and trials seems counter-intuitive, but it is vital. You see, once you get to know the One who has already experienced all the temptations and tests, you can learn to enter into rest knowing that He's got it—*all of it!* Hebrews 2 assures us that although Jesus doesn't give help to angels, He does help those who are the seed of Abraham (children of faith) (Heb. 2:16). That is us. When circumstances, trials and even people come against us, when we are overwhelmed, tested, scrutinized and judged, we can rest knowing that Jesus took on all of our sufferings so that He could offer us relief and come to our aid. Whether we allow Him to or not, however, is up to us. Entering His rest is a choice, an act of our will. It won't happen accidentally or by chance—we must purposefully choose to enter. We must, like Abraham, consider the situation, the big, ugly facts, and then consider them not. In other words, don't let them determine our attitude or our results! The most important thing we can learn is to enter into rest. This is the place of faith, where we have become so intimately acquainted with Him and His Word that we can immerse ourselves in confident and peaceful stillness and abide under His shadow (Ps. 91:1). Rest is contrary to all the world teaches and something we must, on purpose, learn (Matt. 11:28–30). Oh how God longs for us to cry out to Him so that He can teach us! When we learn to place our trust completely in God, then He is able to do the miraculous on our behalf. We don't need to fret or struggle, rather we need to just rest in Him, knowing that He is on our side and He is faithful.

As we close this chapter, let's pray this prayer together:

Lord, we come to you, asking that You would teach us to rest, to trust in You above anything else we feel, see or encounter. Show us how to come to the place so that we know You and experience Your goodness in a way that outshines any "fire" that Satan can set in our lives. As we draw close to You, hide us underneath Your wings, and let us learn to remain there, in you place of protection and provision, in Jesus' name.

Chapter 2
Running on Empty

Our lives are so busy, cluttered with obligations and appointments. This makes us feel incredibly fast paced: causing us to become worn down, weary and even exhausted at times. While this pace can be sustained for brief periods, often thanks to adrenaline and sheer willpower (and enhanced by caffeine), our bodies were not designed to function at such levels of stress over long durations.

In fact, stress (self-induced or otherwise) has been found to be a cause of both physical and mental diseases. When stress levels hit a certain threshold, our systems actually cease to function properly and we become overloaded, which can lead to a breakdown. I personally have experienced a time in my life when I had several "seizure-like" episodes, in which my autonomic nervous system hit the "off" button, causing me to end up in the hospital and to have a series of tests (MRI's, EKG, EEG, CT scan) in an effort to determine why I was experiencing seizures. What a scary thing! Our bodies are designed to protect us, and they are designed to take extreme measures if necessary.

What should we do to make our lives (and stress levels) manageable? Mark 6:31 gives us the answer; the disciples had become so busy, and their attention was so in demand, that they didn't even have time to eat. Jesus instructed them to "Come aside by yourselves to a deserted place and rest awhile" (Mark6:31 AMP). What is the cure for stress, according to Jesus? Time alone resting: away from phones, emails, texts and social media. Acts 3:19 tells us that when we seek the Lord, and repent of taking our focus off of Him from being distracted, stressed out and overloaded, we will become refreshed by His presence. Now this is how we were created to live.

Of course, we've all been in a situation that seems impossible, and where we feel broken-hearted and stressed out, because there seems to be no good answer and no way out. Even Jesus experienced this; in Matthew 26:38, we learn that His soul was "exceedingly sorrowful, even to death." It was then that He asked His disciples to stay with Him and watch (be vigilant, awake and alert).

I'm so glad to have Jesus as my example of "staying power." When the going got tough, He got closer to His Father and prayed and fellowshipped with Him (Matt. 26:39, 42, 44); asking for His will to be done. Jesus knew that He would not only receive direction, but strength to carry Him through His assignment. Despite the desperate situation, He was able to enter rest by being in His Father's presence. He urged His disciples to do the same, so that they could endure the changes and upheaval that His crucifixion would bring.

Unfortunately, they chose to sleep (a state of unconsciousness and inactivity) rather than enter into rest (an active state of waiting, a position of ease and quietness), which cost them peace in the days and weeks following. Jesus is our model for dealing with stress and upset. He is our Great High Priest, and He knows exactly how we feel (Heb. 4:15). Let's take His advice and come boldly to Him to receive the mercy and grace that we need.

Let's imagine that you are setting out on a journey. It would be foolish to begin a long hike with an empty canteen. In the same manner, you would never want to use a canteen that leaked, for when you needed the water, it would not be available to quench your thirst and give you the hydration necessary to survive and to finish your journey. Yet in life, many of us embark on our journey without God, the Living Water, or in a state where we are too broken to be sufficiently filled. The Bible declares in Jeremiah 2:11 that even believers are guilty of this. God tells Jeremiah that His people (those who have called on His name, i.e. believers) have changed (altered, disposed of, exchanged, removed) their glory for what does not profit. In other words, we have traded God's glory (His manifested presence in our lives) for a man-made alternative that may seem similar but because it is a counterfeit, it has no power or benefit in our lives. This is what the Word describes as having a form of godliness while denying (contradicting, rejecting, refusing) God's power (2 Timothy 3:5). In fact, this verse clearly instructs us to turn away from these things. Jeremiah goes on in verse 2:13 to explain exactly what is happening—God's people have committed two evils: 1) they have forsaken (failed, left, refused) God, the fountain of living water, and 2) they have made for themselves cisterns (containers) which are broken and don't hold water. Clearly, this is a very deceived position. They will begin their journey believing that the water (His presence) that they need to sustain life along the way is readily available to them, only to find out when they attempt to access it that their containers are false and hold no provision. This situation is life-threatening. What is the solution to this predicament? The Living Water that Jesus offers to the Samaritan in John 4. We must, as believers, make sure that we equip ourselves with the River of Living Water that never runs dry. How can we do this? By abiding in His presence daily, fellowshipping, studying, and learning from Him. Only in this way will we become containers of His glory and have the supply that we need to complete the journey of our destiny in Him.

Let's face it—life can be draining. The endless demands of work, family, and yes, even religious activities, can lead us to feel fatigued, stressed out and exhausted. The pace doesn't seem to let up and at times it can make you feel like you are a hamster on a wheel, running and running but getting nowhere fast. Where can you run for respite and for shelter and renewal? There is only one Person who is immune to the weariness of the world. Isaiah 40:28–31 reminds us of this fact. The prophet paints a vivid picture of just how powerful, loving and compassionate our God is. The Creator of the universe is never faint (tired) or weary, and His understanding is beyond searching. Now this is Who we need to get hooked up with when we feel like we are running on empty. How can we make sure that we are connected so that we experience His greatness in our lives on a continual basis? The key is in waiting upon the Lord. Isaiah 40:31 declares that the one who waits (binds together with) upon the Lord is the one who renews in strength, mounts up (stirs up) and is able to run and walk. Any need we have, under any condition imaginable, is taken care of and provided for by our God and King. As we press into His presence, abiding with Him on a continual basis, we experience unexplainable strengthening and peace, for a three-fold cord is not quickly broken (Ecclesiastes 4:12).

Of course, we all experience times when it seems impossible to accomplish everything that needs to get done and maintain our joy and sanity in the process. Hebrews 12:1–2 gives us the answer. It instructs us to lay aside (put away, cast off, lay down) every weight (load and burden causing us to bend under it, hindrance) that ensnares us and to run the race that is set before us with endurance. How can we do this? We do this when we only have eyes for Jesus and when we give Him our undivided attention while turning away from all the distractions. Peter was able to step out of the boat (natural realm) and do the miraculous as long as he kept his focus on Jesus (Matthew 14). But as soon as Peter looked at the circumstances around him (the wind and the waves) and took his focus off Jesus, he began to sink. If we keep our focus on Jesus, we will never sink. He is able to bring the victory every time, in every situation. Learning to abide in Him, getting to really know Him by His Word and through prayer is the key. He won't ever leave you when times get tough and you are ready to call it quits. He will be there to help you walk on the top of every wave when the storm is blowing.

The devil is a master of the bait and switch game. For every benefit or blessing the Lord has, the enemy has a counterfeit. Rest is no exception. Amos 6:1 tells us that woe will come to those who are at ease in Zion and to those who trust in Mount Samaria. The prophet is talking to the people of God (Mt. Zion) who have been deceived and trust in the world (Mount Samaria) and its way of thinking and doing things. He goes on to say that God's people (Israel) sought out the smartest and most famous persons in the nation instead of seeking and turning to the voice of the Lord, the Creator of the Universe. How could this happen? Why would the very people who witnessed the Lord's mighty delivering power as they came out of Egypt turn away? They were deceived and lulled into a false sense of security because they had become enamored of the culture around them. They immersed themselves in the folly and lies of the world and they were misled by "nice people" (if they're nice they can't be wrong. What harm could come from listening to them?). The truth is, whatever you spend time focusing on becomes your reality. Isaiah 5:20 tells us that woe is coming to those who call evil good and good evil. This occurs when we buy in to the world's view instead of God's point of view; when we exchange His truth for lies and when we compromise our beliefs in the name of political correctness. Isaiah 5:21 says that when we do this, we become wise in our own eyes and prudent in our own sight. Don't be deceived by the devil's false rest! The only true rest is found in the Truth of God and in His presence and this is the only rest that will satisfy in the darkness of this present world. From this place, we can trade emptiness for the filling of His presence and shine forth as light in the darkness.

Anything God has, the enemy likes to counterfeit as a means of deceiving people and leading them away from God and His ways. Peace is no exception. Ask anyone what the greatest need is for humanity and you will invariable get the answer "world peace." What a good and honorable goal, right? I've even heard some say we should have "peace at all costs." That can't be wrong, right?! There is a vast difference between man's peace and God's peace. The book of Obadiah talks about the perils of worldly peace. In Obadiah

1:7, he outlines how those in your group, the ones who are "at peace" with you, will force you out of your borders and lay a trap for you without you having any awareness of it. All the promises and treaties in the world can't prevent your "allies" from deceiving you, especially if they are given over to unregenerate minds and rebellious and lawless hearts. They may appear to be friends, but their hearts are darkened and evil. This verse says that the very ones who ate bread with you will prevail against you and you won't even know it until it's too late. How can we avoid the tricks and traps set for us by our cunning enemy? Abide in the Lord's presence and let His Word abide in and saturate us (John 15). When we do, He is able to lead us and point out the traps and pitfalls laid before us. What appears good can be exposed in Truth, allowing us to escape. Obadiah verse 1:17 tells us that on Mount Zion (in His presence) there shall be deliverance and holiness. When we purpose to seek the Lord, we find Him to be faithful. He rewards those who diligently seek Him (Heb. 11:6).

As Christians, we need to place our confidence in people and things mindfully. God desires for us to come to Him, to place our trust in Him and to confidently rest, letting Him guide us (Proverbs 3:5–6). We are not to trust our own understanding, but rather to acknowledge Him. Likewise, we, as believers in Jesus Christ, we are not to trust in anyone or anything other than the Lord. Why? Because people and their ways will fail. They are finite entities with limited power and knowledge that cannot fulfill our needs. Yet, it seems that most often, people, even believers, choose to place their trust in things that are man-made. Jeremiah 2:32 declares that God's own people have forgotten (are oblivious of) Him for days without number. His own people! It seems strange that those who call Him Lord would choose to reject Him and His opinion, power and guidance, and instead trust in the natural realm, but it happens every day. What are the results of this? Jeremiah 2:37 states that the Lord has rejected their trusted allies, and that they won't prosper in them. In other words, it is futile to trust in the natural. Our hope, as believers, needs to be firmly grounded in the Lord, Who is our true Refuge and Fortress (Psalm 91). When we choose to truly know Him, entering into the secret place of His presence and abiding there, we can confidently trust that our victory is secure in Him.

The book of Micah reveals that there will be false prophets who come and deceive God's people. They are looking for those who are weary, distracted and self-absorbed. These prophets will cause people to stray from the Truth of the Word and believe a lie. How could this happen? There are two main reasons: a lack of knowledge of God's Word and a desire for comfort for their flesh. Hosea 4:6 warns that God's people are destroyed for lack of knowledge. Why does this happen? This happens because they reject the Truth of His Word. Have you heard phrases like this: "The Bible is outdated" and "Times have changed, and we have progressed"? Beliefs like this are a rejection of His precepts and lead even the church into deception, which in turn leads to destruction. The enemy lives to confuse and ensnare believers, and this is easy to do when we do not know God's Word and when we aren't spending time studying and abiding in His presence and allowing Him to reveal His Truth to us. When we don't know the Word, it's easy to have it used against us. I mean, what's godlier than believing in peace and love for all mankind? But we must remember that God's love leads to repentance, not tolerance of or acceptance of sin. Jesus Himself said that He didn't come to send peace but a sword (Matt.10:34). In other words, He came to bring Truth that would bring His believers into a position diametrically opposed to the world view that surrounded them. This is not typically a comfortable position for our flesh—it takes work to stand against the rising tide of deception and anyone knows it's easier and requires less effort to "go with the flow." Both Micah 3:5–6 and Jeremiah 14:13–14 tells us that these "prophets" (i.e. leaders, even in the church) will stand up and proclaim peace, abundance, and well-being. In fact, they will "assure peace" but it will be a lie. How can we guard against being deceived? The way to spot a counterfeit, to identify a lie, is to study and know the truth backwards, forwards, inside and out. As His children, we must stay full, not empty, by abiding in Him and letting His Word abide in us (John 15:7). We must walk so closely with Him that no enemy and no lie can step in between us. When we do, despite what goes on around us, we will experience true peace and rest, because He is the Word (John 1:14) and He is our Prince of Peace (Isa. 9:6).

During the time that the prophet Micah was alive and speaking, Israel was being seduced by the world around it. They ("the church") had let Canaanite practices and idol worship creep into their lives and into their worship, displacing the God who created them. Sound familiar? Instead of seeking after and trusting the One who created them, they ran after every new doctrine they heard and followed many false gods. God, in His mercy, warned them of the consequences of their behavior, just as He does today. Sin and compromise lead to judgment and destruction. In fact, God stated this plainly in the book of Micah. In Micah 2:10, He warns the people to arise and depart, because what they are involved in is not for them and will only bring destruction. The word arise actually means to abide, be clearer, decree, endure, help, remain, ordain, perform, rise up against, stand up and strengthen. It does not mean "getting up." Rather, it is a call to *stand for* God's Truth, even when everyone around you is compromising. Once the people (church) arise, they are to depart. In other words, once they stand up and declare the Word, they are to depart from sin and deception, growing and prospering along the way as they lead others out of the snare of the enemy. False rest is dangerous because it brings destruction and defilement, disqualifying the people of God from the promises of God. The solution? Repenting and returning to Him and His ways and abiding in His Word and His presence. If we do this, then we will be on the right path, our King will pass before us and lead us in triumph (Mic. 2:13).

"Religion" will tell you that you can be close to Jesus by keeping its tradition, saying what you've always said (even if it praises Him) and doing what you've always done (even if it's the "right" thing). But there comes a time when, if you want a true, deep relationship with the Lord, you have to push past following "religion" in order to truly know Him. Without knowing Him, you cannot enter His rest, and you will remain forever empty. Jesus explained in Matthew 15:8–9 that although the religious people seemed to be doing and saying all the right things, they were falling short in that their hearts and were not truly seeking Him. Believe me, I have been there, and it is awful and empty. I've experienced times in my life when I was involved in as many as 5–6 ministries, being at the church 7 days a week, but feeling dry, exhausted and utterly outside of His presence. Not that serving at church is bad or wrong, in fact it is right to serve Him by serving the body of Christ. But when we are so caught up in "doing" rather than "being" in His presence, we can quickly feel disconnected and discontent. In Matthew 15, Jesus went on to say that their efforts were foolish, unsuccessful and served no purpose (Matt. 15:16). Why waste time and effort for something that ultimately falls short and is worthless? In the words of Jesus, God Himself is interested only in those who will worship Him in spirit and truth

(John 4:23–24). In other words, He does not recognize false or feigned intimacy, but rather searches our hearts for true, sincere, and dependable worship. It is our responsibility as believers to find out how to become intimate with Him in worship and to cultivate this intimate relationship with Him, for out of this secret place flows all we need to become all He has called us to be.

What do we do when we have journeyed long and are empty, weary from the road? Weariness is a sure sign that we need rest. Weariness is more than simply fatigue—it's a lack of strength, energy, and freshness; it is being bored, annoyed, lacking patience and tolerance; in a word, it is exhaustion, both mental and physical. When we continue to live our day-to-day life (work, play, family, church obligations, etc.) without stopping to spend time in His presence, we fail to rest, which leaves us running on empty, in a state of utter depletion. Is it any wonder we feel anxious, agitated and overwhelmed? God's answer is simple: "Come to Me ... and I will give you rest" (Matt. 11:28). When we spend time with Him, He will teach us how to operate from this place of rest, which is where we find everything we need to face every situation in life (Matt. 11:29–30). Whether we come or not, however, is our decision. Did you know that it upsets God when we refuse to enter into His rest? In Hebrews 3, Paul is quoting from Psalm 95 and says that God was angry with the generation who came out of Egypt. Why was God so upset and grieved with the people He mightily delivered from the hand of Pharaoh? He was angry because "(they) always go astray in their heart and they have not known My ways." Let's look at this more closely. To go astray or err means to roam from safety, truth, or virtue, and to deceive, seduce, or wander. The word heart is the word the Greeks used for the very center of one's being, the true self, the thoughts, feelings and mind. It is the spirit of man. In other words, the children of Israel were disregarding God and refusing to follow after the means that God was using to guide them on their journey of deliverance and blessing from the oppression of Pharaoh to the bounty of the Promised Land. They thought their way was better than God's way. What did this attitude of rebellion and "I think my way is better" cost them? Everything! Most importantly, they did not enter His rest—they were unable to settle down and cease from their striving and colonize in His presence. Without this, they were unable to experience and receive all the blessings God had for them. So it is with us today. It seems foolish, but how many times do we vex the Lord with our attitudes, by refusing to allow ourselves to accept and be led by His way of doing things because we don't *feel* He understands? Entering His rest and receiving the fullness of His promises is more than merely an exercise in mental ascent. It is a lifestyle of remaining in the center of His word, His will and His ways, where we find safety, truth and virtue. When we choose to diverge from His path, we can be seduced and deceived by the enemy, forfeiting all He has provided for us.

The word defiant, as used in Jeremiah 5:23, means to turn away, withdraw, backslide, be stubborn or rebellious. The prophet uses it in conjunction with the word rebellious to describe the condition of the hearts of the people of God during his time. In fact, he declares that the people have revolted and departed from the ways of God. This sounds familiar, doesn't it? Jeremiah 5:31 gives us an even clearer picture of what was going on. The prophets and the priests had taken the Lord out of the equation, turning from His ways and His guidance, yet they maintained the framework. The priests still had services, the prophets still declared, "thus says the Lord," yet they were not in line with Him. This is what scripture refers to as having the appearance of godliness while denying its power. We, as believers, are cautioned to turn away from such things (2 Tim. 3:5). A hallmark of the last days will be that we choose to heap teachers on ourselves according to our own desires while not enduring sound doctrine (2 Tim. 4:3). When we cease investing in our relationship with our Father and neglect having time in His presence studying the Word and praying, we easily drift into error and into desires of our flesh and have impure motives. It is our fallen human nature to do so.

The bottom line or the "take away" from all this is that we can depend on God 100 percent of the time. No matter what the situation, we can bring our weary, empty selves to His throne and crawl up into His arms, while we listen to Him tell us "I've got this." It is such a wonderful thing not to have to worry and be stressed out when things come against our health, our finances, our relationships or any other area of our lives. We can be still and know that He is God, and the He is taking care of every aspect, every single detail. Now that is rest.

Let's Pray:

Father, I'm asking You to forgive me for the times that I've been "running on empty," living out of my flesh, my intellect, my ability rather than turning to You, the Author of Life and Source of all that I will ever need. I ask that You help me to be aware of every distraction that the enemy would bring across my path and help me to choose to stay plugged into Your presence rather than the culture of the world. I need more and more of You—fill me up I pray, in Jesus' Name.

Chapter 3

Invitation

Have you ever been invited to a party or other event and thought, "I have so many other things to do. This doesn't seem like a good use of my time"? In our fast-paced world, there are always a multitude of things clamoring for our attention—job requirements, children's activities, deadlines and hobbies. It is a never-ending parade of commitments that can be overwhelming at times. Luke describes people in similar situations. They were invited to a party but each had other things vying for their attention—new wives, land purchases, a new car (OK, technically it was oxen, but you get the picture) (Luke 14:15–20). Each had seemingly legitimate reasons to decline the invitation. Unfortunately, none of them realized that it would cost them the Kingdom (their very salvation). The story goes on to say that the host told his servant to make sure that the banquet was full, so he brought in the poor, maimed, lame and the blind. These folks apparently were excited that they had been asked and they did not have more "pressing" obligations. Think about how many times we feel the tug of the Holy Spirit to come away and spend time in the presence of God and in His Word but we excuse ourselves to do "more important things" like catch up on our favorite TV series, clean the house or mow the grass (I'm guilty as charged on more than one occasion). It is not that other things aren't necessary or important, but the summons of the King outweighs them. We cannot let ourselves become like Martha (Luke 10:38–42), so distracted by the tasks before us that we miss our invitation to have intimate time with our Creator, resting in His presence. It is when we accept His invitation and come away with Him that we receive all we need (strength, peace, ability) to accomplish what has been set before us. We have a daily decision about whether or not to say yes to His invitation.

Our culture has a knack for loading us down with burdens. Things that were meant to be beneficial or bring pleasure or ease can feel like they have a strangle hold on us. Recreation becomes work and schedules become unmanageable. We were never designed to live in a manner where we are continually overburdened, fatigued, anxious, and stressed out. Jesus gave us the remedy to our overloaded, stressed-out lives in Matthew 11:28–30. He says that if we would come to Him (we must take action) with our worries, stress, weariness and problems, He will exchange them for rest. Our job is simply to *come* and He takes care of the rest.

His yoke (serving Him) is easy and the burden (cost) is light. When we choose to come to Him, we will find rest in that place. Why would we choose to do anything else?

Unfortunately, sometimes it seems too easy. Many Christians are striving, but for the wrong things. They may believe that they can "earn" a place in heaven or that they somehow need to push themselves into a position here on earth, whether it be in ministry, their jobs or relationships with others. God is interested in us striving for only one thing and that is to enter in and walk in His will. In Luke 13:24, we see Jesus speaking about the "narrow gate." He tells us to strive to enter by this way because later many will wish they had, but would be unable to. "Strive" in the Greek translation means to compete for a prize, endeavor to accomplish something, fight, or labor fervently. In other words, we are to put all our strength and focus toward entering in by the way He chooses. Why? Because the gate is "narrow" due to obstacles standing close to it. He states that many will not be able to enter around the obstacles. They will not be of strength, have the force to prevail or be whole to do so. He goes on to say that they will then call to Him and tell Him all the "things" they did in His name, including hearing Him teach, but His answer will be "Depart from Me, I didn't know you." How sad to use one's effort but find out it was for the wrong cause! This is why Jesus took the time to explain Martha what the one necessary thing was (Luke 10:38–42). God wants our efforts to be in drawing close to Him, learning

Invitation

His Word and soaking in His presence, not in being distracted by any number of other tasks. When we do this "one thing" He will equip us to do everything else He has called us to do to serve in His Kingdom.

Did you know that how close we get to God and the type of relationship we have with Him depends on us? He wants nothing more than to have intimate fellowship with us, and He created us just for that express purpose. He also created us with free will, however, which He will not override. James 4 declares that if we will draw near to God, He will draw near to us. In order to draw near to the Holy God, we must cleanse our hearts. In other words, to approach God, who is completely holy and righteous, we must search ourselves and repent, turning from the sin of this world. As we do, we need to purposefully set ourselves apart so that we may be used for His purpose. Part of this process is humbling ourselves in the sight of the Lord by turning from pride and selfishness and our own desires. When we do, He promises to lift us up (James 4:10). God wants more than anything to have a close relationship with us, but He instructs us to seek (pursue) Him and to call (invite) Him (Isa. 55:6). This suggests that there is a time when He is not as near or ready to fellowship with us and that there is a time when He will be unavailable. The Bible clearly states that we do not know what tomorrow will bring, that our life is a vapor and could end quickly, without our foreknowledge (James 4:14). When that happens, it will be too late to draw near. But, if we take the opportunity to seek Him and call on Him while He may be found, to forsake our wicked ways and unrighteous thoughts and return to the Lord, His promise to us is that He will have mercy on us and pardon us abundantly (Isa. 55:7). We can't afford to wait to draw near to our Father. There is so much to be gained from intimacy with Him and so much to lose if we continue to ignore His promptings.

So what do we have to do to accept our Heavenly Father's invitation? Rest is an active process, not merely a cessation of work. Hebrews 4 speaks about entering into his rest. Objects that are stationary never move, so they can never enter in. I'm not speaking of striving or working; rather, I'm speaking of a conscious effort on our part to deliberately seek Him, study His Word and pray. This is the key to entering into rest and having a real relationship with God. When we fellowship with Him daily we are making the choice to be welcomed into the secret place where we can be refreshed in His presence. It is in this place where we can go deeper and get to know Him. There is a difference between knowing and *knowing*. We can know facts and information about any person, thing or topic. But when we take the time to develop a relationship with something or someone, our depth of knowledge changes. It comes out of our head and affects our heart. We no longer just have facts we can relay, we have truth we can impart—and truth always trumps facts! In Mark 12:24, Jesus tells the scribes and Pharisees (arguably the most-learned people of His time) that they are deceived

Invitation

because they know neither the scriptures nor the power of God. This was a shocking comment. How could this be, since their lives were spent studying and memorizing scripture? They were the authorities. However, they had missed the one thing that truly would have brought them knowledge—a revelation of the Lord. They had "head" knowledge of the scriptures but could not see the scriptures were not merely facts to be memorized but were truly alive and vital for life. They missed out on having their lives radically changed because they could not comprehend and therefore denied the miracle-working power that was right under their noses. How sad! Let's not make the same mistake. Take time to immerse yourself in His Word, which is Jesus Himself. Get intimately acquainted with His presence and watch as his might and ability show up in your life.

Everything that appears good or appealing isn't beneficial. Have you ever had something "call to you"—an invitation that looks harmless, but in the end comes back to bite you? I'll use the example of food. At one time or another, we've all eaten what we knew we shouldn't, what wasn't good or healthy for us. I heard the story of a coworker who went to a buffet while out of town visiting with her sister. Her sister has been diagnosed with lactose intolerance. While at the buffet, she got a serving of ice cream with all the toppings: whipped cream, sprinkles, hot fudge sauce. Now, you might be saying, "wait a minute, she's lactose intolerant! She is headed for trouble!" Would it surprise you to learn that she *planned* on eating ice cream? And that in fact that was the reason they decided to eat at that particular restaurant? It was indeed the case. While eating the first few bites, she admittedly began feeling the rumbling in her stomach and knew that it would be but a few short minutes before she had to visit the nearest bathroom. When my coworker asked her why she had eaten the dessert despite knowing that it would cause her intestinal distress and pain, her sister replied "but it tastes so good!" She willingly indulged in something she was allergic to because her brain and taste buds were convinced that it was worth it. Eating the wrong thing has consequences. Not only might it make us feel sick or bloated at the time, but it also might leave us with a craving for more. Despite the fact that our flesh likes the taste and wants more junk food, this type of diet can't sustain us or provide the nourishment we need to be strong and healthy. In fact, the steady consumption of such high-sugar, high-fat and nutritionally challenged food leaves the body weak, deficient and prone to disease. Sin is the same way—it may feel good for a time but it places us on a dangerous road moving away from God and His Word, our source of life and health. Just like junk food, sin promises satisfaction that it can't produce. Once it is "consumed" not only do you feel guilty (at least at first), but you are left with an appetite for more. Soon you find that you have drifted away from health and happiness and don't like the way you look or feel. Isaiah speaks of this in chapter 55, verse 2, when God poses this question through him: "Why do you spend money for what is not bread and your wages for what doesn't satisfy"?

The devil's design is to keep you chasing after things that occupy your time, resources, and attention but never feed or fill you. God tells us emphatically to listen carefully to Him and to eat what is good. The Lord never offers us something that will harm us or cause sickness or poverty in any area of our lives. Instead, He feeds us what we need to succeed, to grow and to flourish. In fact, Isaiah 55:3 goes on to say that when we eat what is good, our souls will delight in abundance. There is no lack of provision in Him. When we incline our ear and come to Him, the by-product is that we can hear and our souls will live. Then we can partake of His everlasting covenant and sure mercies. Abiding and feeding on His Word and His faithfulness sure has its benefits!

That God is great, all-knowing, gracious, all-powerful, holy, and full of compassion is well-established in His Word and works. But how can we approach such a God and access all the He is and desires for us? First and foremost, we must be born-again and washed in the blood of the Lamb, Jesus Christ (1 Pet. 1:18–19; 1 John 1:7–9; Heb. 9:12, Rev. 1:5, John 3:5–7). But we can't stop there. We must draw near to Him so that He will draw near to us; we must repent and purify our hearts, submitting to His Lordship in our lives (James 4:7–8). And, we must learn to wait upon Him, resting in His presence. Everything we need is found in Him and is accessed through His presence. Isaiah confirms that from the beginning, He alone has been God and that He acts for the one who waits for Him (Isa. 64:4). In fact, He promises to meet those who rejoice and do righteousness, those who remember Him in His ways (Isa. 64:5). Waiting on our part, therefore, precedes action on God's part. Again, we are not talking about passive, lazy "killing time" waiting, but rather a posture of intimate fellowship, actively pressing in to learn about Him and be transformed. It is in this state where we can access fully His provision and renew our strength (might, ability, capacity to produce). We can then run and not grow weary and walk and not grow faint (Isa. 40:31). Accept His invitation and press in to God; let Him act on your behalf—you will be amazed at the results.

That being said, wouldn't you love your level of peace to be multiplied? God's Word tells us that this is not only possible, but it shows us through what means. 2 Peter 1:2–3 demonstrates that both our peace (prosperity, quietness, rest, wholeness) and our grace (divine influence, enabling, favor) can be multiplied. How can this be accomplished? The answer is through our knowledge of God and Jesus, our Lord. In other words, the more we get to really know God and His Son, Jesus Christ, and the more we take time to investigate His character and His ways of doing and being, the more we will abound in His peace. In addition, He will increasingly equip us to fulfill all He has called us to do. Our provision is found in truly getting to know Him and in spending time with Him. 2 Peter 1:3 goes on to say that His divine power (miraculous power, ability, might, abundance, strength) has given us *all* things that pertain to life and godliness. How? Through the knowledge of Him who called us through His own glory and goodness. Our God is so good that He gives us everything we need to live a powerful, miraculous, successful and godly life full of His ability and empowerment, full of prosperity, quietness, rest and wholeness. And the means of attaining this is by knowing Him and taking the time to learn from Him and about Him so that we can discern, recognize and acknowledge His ways. I'm so glad that He makes all He is available to us, simply through fellowship with Him. He could have made things much harder for us to attain, but God graciously left the "cookies on the bottom shelf" so that whosoever seeks Him can find Him and set in motion His peace and provision in every area of life.

So, how does this translate to our day-to-day life? How can we ensure that we are taken care of when winds blow and scarcity arises? Is there a place where we can run which provides us access to the resources that we need and the protection we crave? I'm glad you asked. The book of Jeremiah is clear when it declares who will be blessed (as well as who will be cursed). Jeremiah 17:7–8 declares that those who trust in the Lord will be blessed. How blessed will they be? They will be like trees planted by the water, spreading out their roots by the river. In other words, they will have stability and a firm foundation and be situated so they have ready access to the source of provision. For this reason, they won't fear when heat comes. They will also not be anxious in drought (lack). They will yield fruit. What an awesome testimony and heritage for those who purposefully choose to make God their refuge. However, Jeremiah is also very clear about those who choose not to make the Lord their refuge, even through passively failing to make a choice. Chapter 17 declares that those who do not choose the Lord are cursed. Why? Because they trust (find refuge, confidence, boldness, security) in man, making the flesh (body, *self*) their strength. Instead of turning to God, these people have hearts that depart from the Lord (Jer. 17:5). How does this happen? I don't believe that most who turn away and begin trusting in other things are openly rebellious or declaring disdain or hatred of God. Rather, I believe that it is much subtler. They begin trusting in their own intelligence, strength, wealth and abilities. They begin considering their circumstances rather than the One who is above every circumstance. The enemy employs this strategy to cause a gradual drifting away. Like an unmoored boat, it takes awhile before anyone notices it has drifted. This is because we often judge based on appearance and by what our senses or emotions tell us. God doesn't use this type of information to judge our position. Instead, He searches (examines intimately) our hearts. He tries the mind in order to give us the fruit of our ways (Jer. 17:10). God is interested in the heart of things—the real deal, not just the appearance. Whether we choose to trust in ability, money, or intellect or simply don't choose to make God our refuge, we will receive the consequences of that choice (and *not* choosing is a choice!). So take some time, examine your heart, repent if necessary and choose to put your trust in God, making Him your refuge. When you do, you trade the curse of self-dependence for the blessing only found in God-dependence.

Easier said than done, right?! God, in his gracious wisdom, answered this very question for me during corporate prayer before a Sunday morning service. He spoke to me very simply. I had been studying rest for about six months or so at this time, and had most recently been studying scriptures with the Greek word "eirene" in them. This word means peace, prosperity, rest, and quietness. God very clearly spoke into my spirit that this "eirene" is His "reset button." Wow! What do you do when some tech gadget isn't working properly? You press the reset button (or if you're like me, you call the support hotline guy, who then instructs you to press reset). In the New Testament, the word eirene is often used to denote peace. Peace is only a part of what this word actually means. This peace is like peace on steroids. It encompasses prosperity, quietness, rest and wholeness. In fact, part of the definition means, "to set at one again." As I pondered this, I looked up the definition of the word reset and this is what I found: to move (something) back to an original place or position, to put back in correct position for healing. I can't help thinking that this is God offering us a means of starting fresh, no matter the situation or difficulty we face. When we accept the invitation to enter His presence, into the secret place, we can come to Him and receive the quietness and rest in Him that is necessary in order to refocus, see clearly and start anew on the correct path. When we get alone with Him, we receive His perspective and can then follow the direction that He has planned, one that is always correct, always beneficial and always has the provision we need to successfully complete our journey. So, when you are troubled, confused, overwhelmed, run to the secret place. When we abide in His presence, He resets our perspective, our minds and our attitudes to His path and we can walk in His rest and peace, confident that we are once again headed in the right direction. We can let His peace be our compass.

So what about when you are merely minding your own business and you hear or feel God speaking to you? This type of invitation is typically asking you to do something you hadn't planned on or showing you something you hadn't expected to see. Believe it or not, you are not alone. This is exactly what happened to Amos. He was a sheep breeder and a fruit gatherer (Amos 7:14) when the Lord called him to be a prophet. In fact, the Bible states that God took him. What exactly does this mean? The Hebrew word for took describes the notion of fetching, reserving, sending for, using, or carrying away. This is certainly not something Amos was striving for, planning on or coveting. It only became part of Amos' plan because it was God's plan for him. When we are submitted to God, trusting and seeking after Him rather than making plans on our own, it is then that He can direct our paths (Proverbs 3:5–6). It is then He will reveal to us things we don't know (Jer. 33:3), because we are laying aside our way of doing things and calling upon (inviting) the Lord. He is a Gentleman who will never force us to do things His way—He requires an invitation—not just the initial invitation (salvation prayer), but an ongoing, daily invitation into every area of our lives, in order to exercise Lordship. When we invite Him in, it is then that He will answer us and show us the great and mighty things we don't know. In other words, when we abide, God can communicate supernatural things to us that are both great and mighty. These are things we would have no way of knowing or comprehending by our natural intellect or senses. It is because Amos was seeking God and abiding in His presence regularly that God could speak to him, change his vocation radically and give him prophetic messages for his nation and government officials. God can't speak to and through those who aren't listening to what He has to say. It is also because of Amos' intimate relationship with the Lord that Amos did not buckle under the pressure or rebuke those who opposed the message God had given him to declare. He was sure of his call and able to rest in what God instructed him to do without wavering or being intimidated (Amos 7:14–16). When we make abiding with Him our aim and habit, we will stand steadfast and immovable in the face of every obstacle and opposition.

Make no mistake; God is calling us to prayer, to repentance, and to seek Him. In 2 Chronicles 7:14, God offers us a solution for the darkness and separation that surrounds us as Christians in a fallen world. He addresses believers, those who are called (*invited,* known by) by His name. He pleads with us to humble ourselves. This is a condition of repentance. We must initiate a move toward God, as found in James 4:8. God desires more than anything that we come to Him, but it must be our decision and requires a lying down of self and every sinful thing that it encompasses. In addition to humbling ourselves, we are instructed to pray and turn away from our wicked (harmful, displeasing) ways. These are the ways that don't line up with His ways, those that cause misery, sorrow, trouble and distress in our lives, even if they are considered "good" or acceptable by the world's standards. Once we turn from evil and submit ourselves to God, James 4:14 goes on to declare that God will hear us when we call. Repentance opens the lines of communication so that our petitions can get through to Him unhindered and He can answer in power. What is the result of us as believers following this model? God says He will not only hear but also forgive our sin and heal our land. If ever there was a time that our world needed this, it is now! It is time to seek Him while He may be found (Isa. 55:6–7), to do what only we can and affect the course of the earth with an invasion of His power and glory.

When we don't spend time in prayer and fellowship with God, we are being prideful, telling Him our way is better and we don't need His plan or advice. Often, we are much like the guests invited to the wedding in Matthew 22, who disregarded the invitation to spend time with the Bridegroom, instead choosing to go their own ways. Literally, they departed, separating themselves from the Host, and found that later when they chose to try to come in, they were removed. They missed out on all that was planned for them because they chose their ways over His. Don't miss your invitation! Spend time with God, submit yourself (and your agenda) to Him and hear His voice clearly directing your steps. Revelation 7:10 speaks of salvation (wholeness, deliverance, health, prosperity) that belongs to our God, Who sits on the throne. When we choose to take our place in Him (Christ), we partake of this glorious provision, because it is who He is. Rest, knowing the victory is yours in Christ. His rest is a place of stillness, where we are able to settle down, to quiet our minds and emotions, and to receive strength and direction. It is a place of refreshing and expectancy, a place to trade our weariness for His ability and our stress for His peace. It is, however, a place we must purposefully enter, not one we accidentally stumble upon. We are to seek His presence today and be diligent to enter into His rest.

The world respects and reveres great rulers. Nations will go to war and fight for the Commander in Chief of their armies, not simply for the person, but for what he or she represents. Songs are sung and battles waged for this cause. I believe we, as Christians, are largely unaware of the One we claim to revere. I say this because if we were truly aware of Him and knew Him, there would be an uprising, a mighty battle cry over the trampling of the truths and standards that He, Jesus Christ, the Messiah, embodies and represents. After all, if we really knew Him and truly believed that the Bible is the Word of Almighty God, we would not find it so easy to "go with the flow" of the world and its ever-changing sense of "right." It is not enough simply to accept His invitation to enter in; as believers we need to become acquainted with the One in whom we are to rest. Isaiah the prophet paints a vivid portrait of our Lord in Chapter 9, verse 6. He tells us that a gift, a Child/Son is given. I don't know about you, but the idea of receiving a gift, especially from God, is exciting! The verse goes on to say that the government is upon His shoulders. In other words, He possesses the power to bear burdens and prevail. The empire is His. His name will be called Wonderful, Counselor, Mighty God, Everlasting Father, and Prince of Peace. Now think of it: this awesome Ruler, the mightiest ever known, desires to dwell in us and be known by us. He longs to be in continual fellowship with us by His precious Holy Spirit and speak to us through His Word. What an overwhelmingly amazing offer this is! Why don't more people accept it? It is because they fail to recognize Who He truly is and the power and authority He possesses. If they truly acknowledged Him, nothing would ever be more important than abiding in Him. Don't miss the opportunity to tap into Him, to enter into the secret place of His presence and learn from Him. Listen closely and you can hear His still small voice calling you above the din of the world, calling you to come aside with Him and rest. Relationship has rewards. The last few verses of Psalm 91 (14–16) clearly show the benefits of knowing God personally. When we set our love on Him, we can know His name (position, authority, character). Once we do, He sets us on high; He puts us into a lofty place in which we are safe, strong, and above all *inaccessible* to the enemy. When we are in Him, we enjoy all the benefits of who He is.

Let's pray:

Lord, right now I say yes to Your invitation: yes to drawing near to You; yes to entering into Your secret place of rest; yes to knowing You intimately. Forgive me for the times that I haven't responded to You; for the times I've let other things take precedence over spending time with You in prayer and reading Your Word. I ask that You continue to lead and guide me into a closer walk with You, for You are my place of rest and You provide all I need pertaining to life and living in a manner which glorifies You. In Jesus' Name I pray.

Chapter 4
Yield

Our world teaches us that it is a badge of honor and a sign of maturity and independence to be "self-sufficient" and make our own decisions, based on what's "right" for us. Unfortunately, this mindset robs us of assuming the position which is the most powerful and most beneficial for us. Isaiah 40:31 declares that those who wait upon the Lord shall renew their strength. That promise in and of itself would appear to make waiting on Him a no-brainer. But God doesn't stop there! The end of Isaiah 40:31 tells us that as we wait, we will mount up on wings as eagles, run and not be weary, and walk and not faint. All the provision, energy, guidance, wisdom and power we need for whatever lies before us is found in the waiting. When we purposefully practice intimate fellowship with our God, and come to know Him in all the truth of His character, we are helped beyond measure. We will not feel pressured by the world to be independent or exalt and exert ourselves. Isaiah 49:23 shares that we will know (recognize, perceive, understand) that He is the Lord. Why? Because those who wait for Him will not be ashamed (disappointed, delayed). In fact, even those held captive and preyed upon shall be delivered (Isa. 49:25). You can take His promise in Isaiah 49:25 to the bank! The Lord will contend with those who contend with His children. He promises to save us and save our children. So, the next time you're feeling pressured, remember to pause, take time to come into the presence of the King of kings, and wait. Your victory is at hand!

The Lord doesn't call us to be strong in ourselves, but rather to be strong in Him (Eph. 6:10). We have come to believe we must be strong on our own, mentally and physically, but this leads to a false sense of security and self-reliance and when we encounter resistance or attack we are often left feeling hopeless and helpless. Did we really think we could do it in our own strength? God calls us to be strong through the Master by way of *His* authoritative power. He is the source of true strength. He is the power that helps us overcome every obstacle. How do we access this power? By knowing Him, spending time with Him, and getting His Word down deep within our hearts so it overflows. In a word, we must *abide*. Resting in Him is our place of victory. We can only find true rest when we abandon ourselves to the One who created us. Since it is "He who made us and not we ourselves" (Ps. 100:3), it stands to reason that He has the best plan for us and wisdom that far exceeds what we could ever attain.

If what He has for us is beyond compare, then why is it so hard for us to let go of self—our way, our plans, our desires? It boils down to this—what we don't know scares us. Matthew 17:33 tells us, however, that whoever seeks to save his life will lose (destroy) it. When we continue to live by our own ways, taking things into our own hands by our own strength, we are destined to lose, and lose big. But Matthew 17:33 goes on to say that whoever chooses to lay their life (way) down will preserve it. How, then, do we overcome our fears and die to self? We do this by getting to know Him. Once we know Him truly, we see His character and experience His faithfulness. The Word becomes much more than a reading assignment; it becomes a living promise from the Lover of our souls. Then it becomes easy to relinquish what little control we let ourselves believe we had. It is a relief to stop struggling and scheming, to crawl up into our Father's lap and have a bird's eye view of our triumph in Him.

> "The rest we seek is not a rejuvenation of our energy; it is the exchange of energy: our life for God's, through which the vessel of our humanity is filled with the Divine Presence, where we relax into the all-sufficiency of Christ Himself."
> —Francis Frangipane, from Holiness, Truth and the Presence of God.

The Merriam-Webster Dictionary defines trust as the belief that someone or something is reliable, good, honest, and/or effective. It means having assured reliance on the character, ability, strength or truth of someone or something. In order to have real trust, we must get to know someone and see them "in action." John 15:13 tells us that there is no greater display of love than to lay down one's life for a friend. This is exactly the kind of love that Jesus had for us. He yielded up His own life in order to reconcile us to the Father. The ultimate sacrifice on the cross is proof of His love for us and of His character. He set aside what His flesh and mind would have chosen to follow God's plan. He is completely trustworthy! Galatians 2:20 (AMP) calls us to be crucified with Christ (extinguishing and subduing our passions and selfishness) so that the life we are living in the here and now can be hidden in Him. We can exchange our stress for His rest by allowing our lives to be yielded up to His purpose and plan. This is the posture of rest. In other words, we need to get to the place where we are so hidden in Christ, so thoroughly resting in Him, that we do and say just what He tells us, nothing more and nothing less. Time and time again, we see that Jesus was so in tune with the Father that He didn't make a move or speak a word without His direction. How many of us, upon learning a close friend was near death, would wait two more days before even beginning on the journey to see him? Yet that is exactly what Jesus did (John 11:6). Why? He was waiting for divine guidance, the release from God to go. How much time, trouble and heartache we would save and how much glory we would bring God if we simply waited, in His presence, until we received the command to go or speak (John 12:49–50). When we wrap ourselves up in Him, entrusting all we have and all we are (including our reputation) to Him, we will no longer be bound by impulse or the opinions of others; we will act solely on what pleases Him. This is life lived in the secret place and the result will be evident to all.

In Colossians 3, Paul gives instruction for proper living to the church, the "elect of God." He speaks about everything we as believers and disciples of Christ are to "put on" if we want to be mature in our Christian walk—tender mercies, kindness, meekness, long suffering, forgiveness, and especially love (Col. 3:13–14). He also raises the subject of peace. This is where he changes his wording. Paul doesn't tell us to "put on" peace, but rather to let it "rule" in our hearts. What does this mean? Paul is telling us that we are to let God's very own peace rule (govern, arbitrate, act as umpire) our hearts. Our very safety, protection, healing, and success depends on us letting His peace act as the umpire of our lives. Sounds important, doesn't it? When we choose to enter into His presence we can let this peace have dominion over all our feelings, mind and heart. That means that we let His peace direct what we do, and how we think, react, and speak, we give Him control over the whole works. When we choose to truly relinquish control to the Lord, praying and seeking Him, we gain a freedom that can never be experienced by thinking and doing things our own way.

Why do you think that we in this day and age have such difficulty resting? Not just on the physical side, but in our minds and even in our spirits? I believe it is related to pride. When we operate in pride, we are saying that we trust ourselves, our ability, our intelligence and our power to accomplish something or navigate a situation. This is an extremely dangerous position because it actually sets us up in direct opposition to God. James tells us that God resists the proud but that He gives grace to the humble (James 4:6). It goes on to say that when we submit to God, we are able to resist the devil, who will flee (run in terror, vanish) from us (James 4:7). It seems that God's plan is for us to come humbly to Him and rid ourselves of relying on our capability independent of His capability. Believe me, on our own we are not that capable and surely no match for the devil. When we rely on Him alone, He will clothe us with His ability, might, and authority and will rout the enemy. And it works every time! Isaiah 66:1–2 declares that He will look upon those who are poor (humble, submitted), contrite (remorseful, sorrowful for sin or shortcoming), and who tremble (have reverence) at His word. When we come to God and submit ourselves to His Lordship, acknowledging our need of Him and repenting of our sin, He is delighted to act on our behalf. It is when we are in this posture that we are able to locate and enter the place of His rest (v.1).

These days, everyone is looking to get ahead, move forward, and excel. People spend hours researching up-and-coming technology, attending self-help seminars, and hitting the gym, all to gain a competitive edge. What if there was a guaranteed way to meet every opportunity with your best foot forward and your head and shoulders above the competition? Would you be interested? In Jeremiah 7:23–24, God shares His principles for getting ahead with the prophet and highlights the reason why His people couldn't seem to succeed. In fact, the Word states that God commanded His people to obey His voice and walk in the ways He commands us. If we follow his command, His Word tells us that He will be our God and we will be His people, and all will be well. That is exactly what people are looking for—favor, contentment, success, and acceptance. It would seem that this is a no-brainer. However, the children of Israel (as well as us today) often let one thing get in the way—themselves. Jeremiah 7:24 declares that they did not obey. Why did they refuse to follow Him and obey His commands? The answer is simply pride. Rather than listening to and being shaped by Him, they chose to follow the counsel and dictates of their evil hearts. In a word, they allowed sin into their lives. Rather than abiding in God and allowing His presence to mold and shape them into happy, successful, contented objects of His favor, they chose self-will, following after what their corrupt minds and flesh thought was good. The result was devastating. Rather than moving forward, they slipped backward.

And the same is true for us today. Although we seek and strive for forward motion, success and pleasure, we can never truly experience these things outside of a deep relationship with God. Our time, effort and resources cannot bring about our purpose; only He can do that. As we listen to Him, inclining our ears to His voice and bowing our wills to His purpose, we will find ourselves smack dab in the center of success, acceptance, honor and favor. Why? Because when we do, we rest in the very center of His presence.

What kind of relationship do you have with someone when you continually ask him or her for help and advice, but never put that wisdom into practice? Do you have any basis to blame that person when things don't turn out the way you wanted? It seems crazy, but many people say they have a relationship with God, the Creator of the universe, but don't follow His wisdom (the Word) or obey His instruction. Then, in frustration, they blame God, and turn to a quick "fix" from worldly sources. This doesn't make sense. How can we say that we acknowledge Him as supreme ruler, all-knowing and all-powerful, yet fail to take his advice to heart or follow His clear instruction? Unfortunately, this is not a new issue. During the time of the prophet Jeremiah, the kingdom was divided into two nations, Israel and Judah, and neither followed His ways. In fact, in Jeremiah 3, God calls Judah "treacherous," meaning that they were deceitful, unfaithful, and offensive. He had likewise been lamenting Israel's harlotry, their lack of relationship with Him and their consistent bent to seek after other gods and idols. Although this was bad, Judah's acts were worse and, in fact, more treacherous. Jeremiah 3:10 declares that instead of turning to God with their whole heart, the people of Judah turned to Him in pretense. In other words, they had a form of godliness, but it was a put-on and a show. They were playing church rather than being the church. They were like the ones Jesus spoke about in Matthew 7 when He declared, "Depart from Me you workers of iniquity! I never knew you!" He called them lawless (wicked, transgressors, unrighteousness) (Jeremiah 3:23). Why? Because they were using His name, calling themselves Christians and attempting to use His authority illegally, without having a relationship with him. It would be like trying to use someone else's credit card to access their account for your own purpose. This is illegal in the world, and it is illegal in the supernatural realm. God's power, authority, name and blood are for the exclusive use of those who are in relationship with Him, the ones He calls His children. We can see what can happen when we try to use His name without authority by looking at the seven sons of Sceva. They attempted to cast out demons in the "name of Jesus whom Paul preached." They didn't have any relationship with Jesus themselves and it didn't turn out pretty for them (Acts 19:14–16). Instead of calling on Jesus' name illegally, we must acknowledge our iniquity and return to God and obey Him (Jer. 3:12–13). When we choose to dwell with Him, acknowledging His Lordship, we are covered and protected in the secret place. Abiding depends upon our obedience.

One day, God dropped the word "yield" into my spirit. I love the definition of this word! Not only does it mean to surrender, relinquish possession of, and give up claim to, it also means to reward, to profit, and to produce. In Romans 6:16, we learn that whatever we yield ourselves to or relinquish control to becomes our master. Whatever we abide in or spend time with becomes the controlling influence in our lives. And it produces after its own kind. What are you producing in your life? Stress, strife, anger, upset, frustration? Wouldn't you like to trade those things in and produce what God Himself produces: love, joy, peace, patience, kindness, goodness, gentleness, self-control (Gal. 5:22)? When you yield yourself to Him, you have all that is necessary to produce these things in your life. Abide in Him and all His characteristics, and benefits will be produced in your life.

Isaiah 9 gives us a detailed description of God's gift to us. It speaks of Jesus being our "Prince of Peace" (safety, welfare, prosperity, health, favor, rest, wholeness, perfection). What do princes do? They rule! If we allow Jesus to be our Lord, we should have the evidence of His rule in our life and the gift of a peace that passes all understanding. As we keep our minds on Him, He promises to keep us in perfect peace, which can literally be translated as "peace peace." This means doubled and emphasized peace. The Holy Spirit living on the inside of us teaches us to abide in His peace so that we can surrender to His rule in our lives. We obtain this peace by surrendering to His will and submitting to His Word. Isaiah 26:3 goes on to tell us that perfect peace comes from an attitude of trust, where God is our refuge and we are confident, sure, and full of hope in His presence. When we allow ourselves to be under His rule, rest in His peace and trust Him, His power and His presence will bring about His promises in our lives.

In Revelation 14:13, rest is promised to those who die in the Lord. They are called blessed (supremely happy, fortunate, well-off). They no longer have to toil, be weary, experience pain or have trouble. While being one with the Lord in Heaven is a blessing we should all desire, the death this verse speaks of is not only a literal death but also a figurative one. The question, then, becomes how can we, as those who live in a mortal body, experience this "death." The Lord showed me that death to me (my will, my way of doing things, my mindset) is the key to gaining His rest and His blessing. Galatians 2:20 says that when we are crucified with Christ it is no longer us who live, but it is Him living through us. Too often, we stop short of the crucifixion of self because it is anything but comfortable and in the end it results in death to our familiar way of living. Galatians 5:24 tells us that those who are Christ's have crucified the flesh and all of its affections and lusts. Galatians 5:25 goes on to say that if we live in the Spirit, we should also walk in the Spirit. We can't do this while dragging around the corpse of our flesh, much less while fighting with flesh that is still alive and kicking! In order to experience the true rest of God, we must trust Him and willingly put to death the selves that the world has made. There is nothing there worth keeping and the trade-off is beyond compare. All of our broken, dysfunctional ways can be traded for His perfection, peace, joy, and victory.

Have you ever wondered how the men and women of God in the Bible, as well as the ministers of old, were able to perform such awesome feats and miracles? It's not every day that you see someone survive a night with lions in his cage or witness someone hit the water with their shawl, causing it to split so that they can cross a river! Why don't we see more of this today and what was the secret? Of course, not everyone in biblical times experienced these miraculous signs and wonders. Then, as now, it had to do with relationship. Moses knew God first-hand and spent time every day meeting with Him face to face. Daniel prayed and sought God three times a day and received mighty revelation and wisdom. James 4:8 tells us that if we draw near to God, He will draw near to us. But, there is another requirement—humbling ourselves and repenting of those things (actions, thoughts, and motives) that are ungodly and sinful (James 4:8–10). In order to come close to the Holy God, we can't just come any way we want; because He is holy, we must be cleansed. How do we become cleansed? This happens through the blood of Jesus, which makes us righteous and puts us in right standing with God. This, however, is not a casual act to be taken lightly—it is a position He paid for on our behalf. While it is true that the blood of Christ allows us to come boldly to His throne of grace, we cannot do so with a lifestyle of continual sin. We must set ourselves apart and earnestly seek to walk according to His ways and be quick to repent and make adjustments when we fall short. This is what is needed to have continual fellowship with God, to be one "after His own heart." John 15:5 shows us the key to bringing forth much fruit—abiding in Him and letting Him abide in us. Daniel 11:32 tells us that the people who know God shall be strong and do great exploits (exciting acts, notable/heroic deeds). In other words, in order to see the fruit of His power and to display His majesty, His people must be prepared to let His holiness flow through them. We don't have to be perfect, but we must be willing to be perfected. As we turn our hearts and eyes to Him, we become tender and teachable, which are perfect conditions to allow the Mighty One to demonstrate His awesome power through us on this earth.

In His final act on the cross, Jesus presented His spirit, His very life force, into the Father's hands, and trusted Him completely. He is our example. In Matthew 16:24, Jesus told His disciples that if anyone makes a choice to enter in and accompany Him and be His disciple, that person must disown and utterly abandon their own ways. The decision to lay down our own rights and choices allows us to truly follow the actions of our Lord and Savior, making us one of His own. It isn't possible to do this half-way. If we only commit ourselves half-way, we are as deceived as those to whom He said "depart from Me, I never knew you" (Matt. 7:21–23). Instead, like Paul, to be His disciples, we must die daily (1 Cor. 15:31) to our own ways and fleshly desires. When we do, we place our lives in His hands and entrust Him with protecting and keeping us. This is the yielding that God is looking for from His followers.

There is always hope in the Lord. In the book of Isaiah, the children of Israel had been oppressed and enslaved by the Babylonians. But God, through the prophet, assured His people that He had not forgotten them, even in the midst of their darkness and idolatry. In the first verse of Isaiah 14, we see the promise that the Lord will have mercy and will still choose Israel. In fact, despite what things looked like, He promised to turn the situation around so that His children can take captive those who previously held them in bondage. Talk about a turn-around! In Isaiah 14:3–7, Isaiah describes the rest that Israel can enter into because God is on their side and fighting for them. It promises that the Lord will give them rest from sorrow, fear and bondage. As a nation, Israel had fallen into bondage and idolatry through interactions with pagans around them. They incorporated all kinds of idols and rituals into their worship. You might ask what would represent an idol for us today, since few if any of us have wooden or golden statues in our homes. An idol is simply anything that we have made bigger than God in our lives, anything (good or bad) that has taken a position above Him. It's no coincidence that having an idol causes us to experience pain and sorrow in our lives. This occurs because we are out of balance, making it necessary for us to work and toil to "keep things going." This leads to undue stress, fear, anger and upset. But God says to us, "let it go, trust in Me alone. I will have mercy on you and rescue you, releasing you from the pain and bondage of the idols you've set up, if you trust in Me." When we choose to give up our own way and submit to His way, oh the freedom we experience! We are then truly able to rest and be quiet while we allow Him to work on our behalf.

Daniel was given an end-times vision that closely parallels what is currently happening in our nation and world. In chapter 12 of the book of Daniel, we see that "many shall be purified, made white, refined, but the wicked shall do wickedly and none of the wicked shall understand but the wise shall understand" (Daniel 12:10). In other words, it will come to a point where we must choose—darkness and light can have no fellowship. True Disciples of Christ will be purified and refined but the wicked will do wickedly. We need to recognize this and rather than complain or hide our heads in the sand, we must do what Daniel was instructed to do by God. God told Daniel, "go your way till the end. You will rest, and then at the end of the days you will rise to receive your allotted inheritance." The English words used in translation lose much of the meaning of these commands. "Go your way" means to walk, bear, carry, come away, grow, lead forth, march, prosper, pursue, cause to run, spread, or journey. Rather than just walking away and washing his hands of the mess around him, Daniel was to come away with God, to grow, prosper, and pursue Him. Doing so caused Daniel to then lead the way in a God-less nation and spread God's purpose and plan for all to see. He was also told to rest. Again, this does not mean to lie down and do nothing. On the contrary, he was to settle down and then arise. How long was he to actively abide while leading others to do so as well? His inheritance (destiny) was to be at the end of days (forever, continual). God has given us the glorious job of remaining as an occupying army, showing forth His glory and power in the midst of a world growing ever darker, and we need to remain at our post, faithfully praying and abiding in His presence until His return. There is truly no better place and time to be alive as His disciple than now.

God has already made provision for you and me, as His disciples, to live in these dark times and yet shine forth His glorious light. How is it possible in such abject darkness, with racial tensions, the murder and subsequent trafficking of the body parts of the unborn, the advancement and nearly across-the-board acceptance of the Lesbian/Gay/Bisexual/Transgender agenda? Second Peter 2:2–3 holds the answer. Peter proclaims that both grace (His divine empowerment to live a life that's pleasing to Him) and peace will be multiplied to His disciples. How? It will be done through the knowledge of God and Jesus as Lord. In other words, He pours out

His divine resources on those who rest in Him and remain fixed on His position as Lord of their lives. There are those who would protest, arguing that the world is too dark or that it is too difficult to surrender all to His Lordship. Peter's response is that we can access His divine power and strength through our knowledge of Him. We must become intimately acquainted with God and His character, His Word, and His voice through fellowship with His Holy Spirit. It is simply not enough to read a verse of the Bible and pray over our meals. We must have intimacy with the All-Sufficient One, the Creator. We need only to be willing and obedient and He will equip us! He takes His own ability and might and allows us to rest while He leads us into everything we need to be His witnesses here on earth. We need not struggle or be stressed over how He will do this because He works through us as we fully surrender to His Lordship. In the words of Kathryn Kuhlman, "It will cost you everything." The great reward of a life lived in His presence and fulfilling His purpose, however, far exceeds any fleshly sacrifice we could ever make.

God's rest is not merely a concept; it is a destination. Isaiah 28 tells us that God longs to give His people knowledge line upon line and precept upon precept (Isa. 28:9–10). We gain this knowledge through the study of His Word. Romans 10:17 declares that faith comes from hearing the Word of God. When we give audience to His Word and allow the Holy Spirit to speak to us and enlighten our understanding, He will lead us into rest. This rest allows those who are weary from life's trials and circumstances to become refreshed (Isa. 28:12). Unfortunately, most do not hear His call. We must listen as He calls out to us, to come aside and spend time with the Lover of our souls. Only then will we be able to enter into and remain in the destination of rest that He has prepared only for those who choose Him.

In Isaiah 30, the Bible outlines the futility of attempting to find strength and wisdom in Egypt (i.e. the world's system). The beginning of this chapter accurately describes what is going on in our culture today, despite being written nearly three thousand years ago. The majority of society, even those who were once considered believers, have gone astray in rebellion and seek truth where there is none to be found. They live outside the will and Word of God. Instead of seeking God's wisdom and asking advice from the Creator of the universe, we have chosen to run after the counsel of the world, much to our detriment. Many have called for the end of "outdated religious beliefs" (Isaiah 30:10–11). Rather than standing for truth and right, oppression and perversity have become the banners that people fly. How is it possible to recover from such blatant rebellion against God and His ways? We, as disciples of God, must stand fast, and show others the way. Isaiah 30:15 makes it clear that God desires us to return to Him, His counsel and His ways (Isa. 30:1–2). In fact, He tells us that this is the way we shall be saved. Matthew 7:21–23 shows us that it is not merely a simple prayer or going to church regularly that ensures our salvation, but rather an ongoing relationship with God. In fact, this is where rest comes in. It's not enough to return to God's counsel and ways; we must rest there. Abiding is the key. When we as believers enter into a habit of dwelling in His presence and continually fellowship with Him through the Word and prayer, we can show others the way. Isaiah 30:15 goes on to say that in quietness (stillness, rest) and confidence we will have strength. So, trade in the shifting sand of the current world-view for the firm foundation of God's counsel. Make it your daily aim and your lifestyle. Proverbs 3:5–6 promises us that when we trade our natural understanding for rest in Him and trust Him with every life circumstance, He will direct our paths.

I love verse 20 of Romans 16! It says "and the God of peace will crush Satan under your feet shortly." That's a pretty strong statement on our behalf and the image is vivid. I picture it kind of like stomping on an egg and watching how quickly and easily it smashes under my heel, never to be put back together again. The damage and destruction is final. I find it equally interesting that the God of peace is going to do it. We don't often think of peace as an offensive weapon. What do we need to do in order to position ourselves so the God of peace will work on our behalf? Look back a verse and see—we are to be obedient (to His commands) and to be wise in what is good while being simple concerning evil. Read His Word and spend time talking to Him. He sent His Holy Spirit to be our Counselor and Guide. When we look to Him for wisdom rather than the world we are being wise in what is good and simple in what is evil. So, as we seek Him, He will manifest Himself as the God of peace. We gain peace as we do things His way because our spirit and actions line up with His will; and there is no longer a battle going on within us. When we are aligned with His will, it is then that He can fight for us and crush Satan under His feet! So get in position and watch Him work in your situation.

Lord, I ask You to forgive me for the times that I have not yielded to Your will and Your ways, stubbornly clinging to my thoughts, my feelings and my way of doing things. I ask that You would help me to yield, to be molded and shaped under Your loving hands so that I might be a vessel of honor, fit for Your use, in Jesus' name.

Chapter 5
A New Perspective

Anxiety is everywhere in our world. It's easy to fall into the trap of thinking about all of the "what-ifs" in life. It is when we become caught up in such a cycle that we exchange the situation for our Savior, letting fear dictate our day rather than focusing on the God Who says "Fear not, for I am with you" (Isa. 41:10). It's all a matter of perspective! In Mark 13:11, Jesus instructs His followers not to fear or worry, even when they are arrested for the Gospel's sake. He even says not to premeditate what to say when this happens. How is it possible remain calm in the face of this sort of stress and persecution and not rehearse what you might say in advance? Jesus gives us the key: fellowship with the Holy Spirit. He says simply to speak what is given to us in the hour of difficulty and turmoil. In order for us to know what to say, however, we must be communicating with, and listening closely to, the Holy Spirit. We do this by quieting everything around us, purposely spending time in His presence. When we enter the secret place, we can truly "be anxious for nothing" (Phil. 4:6) because it is there that we find all the answers. It is there that we can grab ahold of what is "given us in that hour" and speak it. We don't have to worry about what we will say, because it will not be us speaking but the Holy Spirit (Mark 13:11). What a relief to know that He is not only with us in trials and trouble, but will actually tell us what to say as we rest in Him. And as we listen and repeat what He says, we will look composed, smart, and victorious. Nothing to worry about here.

How, then, can we achieve this change of perspective, to enter the place where we are allowing every situation to be filtered through the eyes and mind of God? Some may ask how it is even possible to have peace in the midst of a time so filled with darkness, struggle, violence and fear. The good news is that God has already provided for humanity, even in the state of depravity in which it now exists. Luke 1: 78–79 tells us that it is because of His tender mercy that He sent Jesus into the world. What was Jesus' job? To shine His light on those who sit in the midst of darkness and the shadow of death (sounds like our world, doesn't it?) and guide us out, into the way of peace. The word peace does not simply mean absence of fighting. In the Greek, it means a state of rest, quietness, calmness, absence of strife, and perfect well-being. This rest will bring us into harmonious relation with not only God, but man, nations, and our families. When we truly know Him, His way of rest will spill over into every other area in our lives! When we follow His lead and allow Him to guide us, we can experience rest even when chaos surrounds us. In other words, we gain His perspective on the whole situation.

In order to see things from God's perspective, we must be able to hear His voice. It is impossible for us to see and hear clearly unless we get into His presence, which is also called "the secret place." Revelation 4:1 speaks of an open door in heaven (in other words prophetic revelation) but states that we need to "come up" and He will "show us things." When we abide in Him and spend time in His presence, we get the heavenly perspective on situations and circumstances because He is seated above all things. The view from the mountaintop is very different and much more far-reaching than the view from the valley. Imagine for a moment that you are a passenger on an airplane that is flying at an altitude of twenty thousand feet. As you look out at the ground below, you see trees, houses, and cars, and they all are miniature-sized! It's not that the homes and cars are any smaller than they ever were, but that your perspective is different. You are above, looking down upon them. From this perspective, it seems like you could reach out and pick up a house or car; that it would fit into the palm of your hand. What a difference perspective makes. God is urging us to come up higher and enjoy the view!

A New Perspective

The Bible instructs us in Philippians 2:5 to have the same mindset as Christ Jesus. This means that we are to have the same attitude, opinions and purpose as Him and we should set our affections on what he does, think about what he thinks about, and interest ourselves in what He is interested in. This is a tall order! In fact, Jesus called Peter, one of those closest to Him, "Satan" in Matthew 16:23, saying that his thinking caused Him displeasure and was a stumbling block which caused others to fail. Whoa! How on earth could this have happened? It happened because Peter was thinking the way world did about the situation at hand instead thinking like Jesus did. He looked to the natural, rather than the supernatural to get his perspective on the issue, which then gave him faulty information regarding how things should be handled. But, you might ask, how can we know what Jesus thinks and get to the place that our minds are changed, to where we are thinking the way He thinks? The answer is: by resting in Him, spending time in His presence, and getting to know His Word, His ways, and His wishes. Only by spending time with Him can we get our thoughts and ways out of the way and move into the realm of His ways.

Trouble has a way of squeezing you, making it seem like you can't catch your breath. It seems like trouble, conflict, adversity and darkness are all around us and pressing in on us daily. It is a fact that as the world grows darker, pressures and troubles will mount, and we as believers must learn to rest in the midst of them. Habakkuk 3:16–19 talks about such a situation. It seemed like everything was going wrong—the economy was bad, there was a food shortage, there was pressure all around, even to obtain the necessities of daily life. It was a time when the world was at war and the threat of invasion by hostile forces loomed ever on the horizon. The poor were oppressed and the legal system had collapsed. What was Habakkuk's prayer amidst the doubt and turmoil? It was simply this: "that I might rest in the day of trouble" (Hab. 3:16). The word used for rest means: settle down, dwell, stay, withdraw, give comfort, cease, quiet, remain. Habakkuk teaches us that we must rest in the midst of trouble (adversity, affliction, distress). How is it possible to do this? It is possible when we take our eyes off of the problems and fix them on the One who is the problem-solver. In fact, Habakkuk purposefully chose to list all the trials and troubles going on (Hab. 3:17). He then said that in spite of it all he chose to rejoice and to experience joy in the Lord, the God of his salvation. If that seems excessive, you don't understand Who your God is! Habakkuk knew that he served the God of his salvation and he had confidence that He could do again what He had done in times past for His people. In other words, Habakkuk was a man who lived by faith. Because he knew God intimately and spent time with Him, he had every confidence in Him and was fully persuaded that He would step in and take care of the situation. In fact, he stated that the Lord was his strength. He believed God was not only capable but willing to stand on his behalf in

A New Perspective

the face of dire circumstances. We, like Habakkuk, need to be fully convinced that we serve the God who is willing and able to fight on our behalf, no matter what comes our way. Then we can say, "we are hard-pressed on every side, yet not crushed, we are perplexed but not in despair, persecuted but not forsaken, struck down but not destroyed" (2 Cor. 4:8–9). When we truly know our God, we can rest courageously, no matter what we face.

We all experience times when our circumstances seem overwhelming, when the onslaught of the enemy seems relentless and we feel distressed, poor, and powerless. It seems like the world system is gaining power and that the people of God are losing ground. But Isaiah, in the midst of all that was happening around him, chose to praise the One who is worthy. Isaiah 25:1 finds Isaiah proclaiming the God he served and exalting Him by praising His name, recounting His wonderful works as well as His faithfulness and truth. Isaiah knew the secret to rest—abiding with God, recounting His goodness and clinging to His promises (the Word). He had experienced first-hand the mercy and grace of God, and when trouble came, Isaiah purposed to rest in His character and strength. In Isaiah 25:3, he proclaims that his enemies, a strong people, will glorify God! Why? Because God shows Himself to be the strength of the poor (dangling, weak, needy) and needy in their distress (Isa. 25:4). In fact, the Word tells us that in our weakness His strength (miracle-working power, ability, abundance, might) is made perfect (complete, fulfilled, finish, accomplished)! It is then that the power of Christ can rest upon the believer (2 Cor.12:9). So, when you are feeling backed into a corner, pushed down and overwhelmed, remember to run toward Him. Abide in His presence and let His miracle-working power be your strength as you lift Him up!

When I was small, my Daddy seemed so big to me. It seemed that there was nothing that he couldn't do. If I needed him to help me learn to ride my bike, he was willing and available. I never doubted that he was able to hold me up and prevent me from tipping over or crashing into the mailbox. He was Dad and he was strong and capable. I had the utmost confidence in him to take care of me and help me in whatever way necessary. In chapter 5 of First John, we read about the confidence we are to have in God. 1 John 5:14–15 tell us that we are to have complete assurance that if we ask anything according to His will, He hears us. We never have to wonder if God is listening. God's Word is true, guaranteed, secure, and free from doubt or uncertainty. This is the confidence we are to have toward God when we pray. How? We can rest in Him and in His ability, His faithfulness, His love and His strength. We never have to wonder if He loves us (John 3:16) or if He will work on our behalf. In fact, part of the definition of rest is to have peace of mind or spirit and to be free from anxiety. When we enter into the secret place and set our expectation on God as the performer rather than ourselves, we are set free from all manner of worry, doubt and anxiety. We are confident in His care for us and His capability to care for us. We no longer need to fret or fear because our Daddy God has got this! He always takes care of us in grand style!

Gaining God's perspective gives us an inside "edge" on every situation. Who doesn't like insider information and being in on something that only a select few know? In Luke 8:10, Jesus told His disciples (those who spent time with Him regularly and followed His teachings faithfully) that it was God's plan to let them in on the mysteries of the Kingdom. In other words, the truths and secrets that were hidden from the masses would be revealed to them because of their relationship with Him. Things that could never be known or grasped by their own natural understanding would be illuminated by revelation from the Holy Ghost. We are the very ones that God wants to reveal His secrets and plans to! Don't go through life wishing you understood what God is saying or wants you to do. Press in to Him, tap into His wisdom and walk in the revelation by which He wants His believers to operate. Jesus spoke to the masses in parables, but He spoke to those who followed Him closely and had a relationship with Him much differently. Mark 4:34 tells us that when the disciples (dedicated and convinced followers) were alone with Him, He explained all things to them. In other words, when those who were faithful, devoted servants spent time in His presence, fellowshipping with Him, Jesus revealed things to them. He didn't speak to them the same way that He did to others; rather, He took time and went into detail, explaining and expounding on the truths He put forth in the parables. Do you want more understanding? How about more revelation knowledge and wisdom? Do you want God's perspective? The key to having all these things is to devote yourself to Him, spend time alone with Him and let Him unfold mysteries to you.

Wouldn't you love to have a fool-proof way to success, a means of getting ahead and achieving in every area of your life? We tend to struggle and spend our energy on the "doing" and the accomplishment of this task or that task, but we would be better off to apply ourselves to the "hearing" (with our ears) first. In fact, this is the key to success in doing anything. I'm not talking about the casual "I'm listening; I've got it" type of hearing but rather the kind of hearing which requires us to draw near. In Isaiah 48:16–19, God is speaking to His people about this very thing. He urges us to come near to Him and hear (pay attention, obey). This is a far cry from the passive posture we typically ascribe to hearing. Isaiah 48:16 goes on to say that He has not spoken in secret. God makes His voice and His instructions clear to those who draw near. In fact, He promises to teach us to profit and lead us in the way that we should go. However, just as in a natural classroom, it is the individual student's choice whether to tune in and pay attention, seeking the training provided, or to tune out, absorbing nothing of the lessons being presented. Also as in a natural classroom, instruction precedes testing, and if the information needed is not learned and then applied, failure is imminent. The teacher who presents effectively is not at fault when the learner tunes out and declines to learn. The benefits of the material are forfeited when we choose not to pay attention to our Teacher by drawing close and hearing what He has to say. Conversely, when we choose to hear His commandments, He promises that our peace will be like a river and our righteousness will be like the waves of the sea (Isa. 48:18).

The key to getting God's perspective on things is becoming intimately acquainted with Him. You wouldn't expect to know what a stranger on the street thinks about the economy, political issues or health care reform, would you? Of course not! But you probably have a very good idea how your spouse or best friend feel about these issues. Why? You know because you are well acquainted with them and spend time in their presence, talking about these kinds issues and so much more. You are confident in your knowledge of their personalities, priorities and preferences. It is no different when we seek to gain God's perspective. We have to spend time with Him, becoming familiar with His ways and character as well as His likes and dislikes. One important way we learn about God is through His Word. Studying the Word is how we become acquainted with our Father God. Spending time in the Word allows us to increase our knowledge and understanding of His will and ways. When we do, we gain understanding of how He operates and what our rights and privileges as His children are. This in turn produces faith; and without faith we are unable to please Him (Hebrews 11:6). The Bible, His Word, declares that Jesus is the living Word of God. In John 8:31–32, the Bible tells us that if we abide in His Word, we are truly His committed followers (disciples). John 8:32 then goes on to say that this causes us to know (understand) the truth that will make us free. In other words, remaining in a relationship with Jesus (the Word) will cause us to have insight and revelation from God.

We see over and over again in the Bible that God is concerned with our peace. In fact, Ephesians 2:14 tells us that Jesus Himself is our peace. If that is true (and it is, because the Word of God is infallible truth), then why do many, if not most, Christians appear to have a lack of peace (prosperity, rest, quietness, wholeness) in their lives? Where is the disconnect? Ephesians 2:14 says that Jesus broke down the wall of separation in order for us to experience peace (as well as all the other benefits of being in Christ). This literally means that He destroyed, dissolved and melted every barrier that might keep us from experiencing all He came to give us through His death, burial, and resurrection! That is great news! He came to declare a peace that is found only in Him to all of us—even those of us who were yet to be born. If Jesus did all this for us, why don't we experience it on a daily basis? It's like owning a house but not using the key. You can admire the house and even tell others about the house without using the key, but you can't experience first-hand the benefits of homeownership until you use the key—it unlocks the benefits. You can enter in, make yourself some food in the kitchen, take a shower, relax and watch TV once you use the key. That's a lot different than standing outside. The key is found not only in becoming intimately acquainted with Jesus, but with the Holy Spirit. It is by the Holy Spirit that we are able to access all the benefits of Calvary (Eph. 2:18). Access is simply a way of getting near to someone or something and having permission to communicate with them. Since Jesus is in Heaven with the Father, the Holy Spirit is the One who has come to be our Helper, Comforter, Advocate and Guide and to abide with us forever (John 14:16). As we take the time to get to know Him intimately, spending time in His presence, He shows us the way to access all the things (even peace) that Jesus provided for us.

So we now know that we must gain access to Him—to know Him intimately in order to gain His perspective and see things as He does. We have to remember this, no matter what the world throws at us at the moment. When everything is going wrong, when injustice and evil seem to be winning, where can we find solace? Where can we run to find rest and peace in the midst of upheaval and unrest? The Bible tells us in Psalm 119:165 that we can find true peace when we love His law. In other words, when we spend time reading His Word, when we value it and focus on it, giving it a place of preeminence in our daily lives, then peace and rest will flood our lives. This is not because the craziness of the world has ceased or because things have suddenly become godlier. It is, rather, a result of our thoughts, actions and lives coming into alignment with God's plans, purposes and mindset. As we spend time studying His Word and acknowledging His truth, God will direct our steps according to His Word, and no iniquity will have dominion over us (Psalm 119:133). In these times of turmoil, we need to turn our attention to God and His Word, for our hope is in His Word, the only thing that will last forever (Ps.119:160, Matt. 24:35). When we do, we have the promise that we will not stumble (be offended, caused to fall). We can remain focused on what He's called us to do, which is to be the salt of the earth and the light of the world. If ever this world needed us to be the light, it is now!

Did you know that positioning ourselves in rest actually brings honor to God? The posture of rest declares to God, to ourselves and to everyone watching that we have fully placed our trust in the Lord to achieve the victory! When the nation of Israel was instructed to leave Egypt, God told Moses that He would harden the heart of Pharaoh and cause the Egyptians to pursue them as they left Egypt (Exod. 14:4–18). God had a purpose for making the Egyptians chase the people of Israel. God wanted to show not only Israel but also Egypt and the rest of the world that no matter how many soldiers, weapons and resources there were and no matter what military or monetary advantage was leveled against His people, they would be no match for His glory and greatness.

You see, God likes to show off on our behalf and this was an example of a divine set up. That being said, not everyone was fully convinced that victory was Israel's. Why? Because as the Egyptian army, with all its soldiers, horses and chariots began to give chase, the children of Israel were influenced by what they *saw.* In other words, they lifted up their eyes and placed the natural above the supernatural. They gave what they saw the glory instead of giving the glory to what God could do. Why? They failed to give Him glory because they did not know Him intimately and therefore they were unable to trust His character and ability. In fact, they accused Moses of taking them to the wilderness to kill them! But Moses, who had a close personal knowledge of God, told the people not to fear the Egyptian army but rather to stand still and see the salvation of the Lord (Exod. 14:13). God desired to show victory on behalf of His people to every adversary as He brought them out of bondage and into His purpose and promise. And He wanted to fight on their behalf while the Israelites held their peace so that He could demonstrate His love, commitment, ability and care for His people (Exod. 14:14). His plans and desires in this regard have not changed—God still wants us to go forward in the face of adversity, resting in our knowledge that He is good and His mercy endures forever (2 Chron. 20:21).

The promises of God belong to His children, but they can only be obtained through faith. Hebrews 4:1–3 tells us that despite having the promise that they could enter

God's rest, most of the children of Israel did not receive this promise because they didn't have faith. In other words, despite having a pledge from God that they could cease from stress and striving and make Him their dwelling place, the promise wasn't advantageous or beneficial to them because they were not fully persuaded. The concept of faith (being fully persuaded) involves a constant profession (continual declaring) of the promise. When we truly believe God is Who He says He is and can do what He says He can do, we will speak it out. We can only make this declaration if we have His perspective on things. It is only then that we, like Abraham, are fully persuaded and can rest in Him, knowing beyond a shadow of a doubt that He is able to make good on His promises (Rom. 4:21).

Faith is not what God does, it is Who He is, the very essence of His nature. You and I can trust Him and rest in Him.

Lord, I thank You that it is possible for me to know You intimately and in the process gain Your perspective, exchanging the one that the world has tried to impart to me for Your perfect vision. I ask that You help me to come to know You more intimately than I ever have, and in doing so, assist me in learning and knowing Your ways, for they are higher than mine, and in You there is no darkness. Your perspective is clear, right and true in every situation, and I submit myself to You, allowing Your precious Holy Spirit to speak to me and guide me in all truth.

Chapter 6
Hiding Place

When I was a little girl (and even when I was not-so-little), and things seemed overwhelming, scary or just plain bad, I had an almost irresistible urge to run away and hide. I wanted to be completely covered so no one could find me. I remember sleeping with dozens of stuffed animals, buried beneath the covers, hidden away. What I discovered is that when I placed things on top of myself in an effort to conceal myself, it got hard to breathe! I would get sweaty, short of breath and miserable, not to mention totally unable to sleep. I believe the urge to hide ourselves is innate, put there by God for our protection and survival. The problem is, we don't use His techniques, but rather take it upon ourselves to figure out how best to hide away. Psalm 32:7 tells us that God is our hiding place. In other words, God Himself is our covering, disguise, protection, and secret place. He preserves (guards, protects, conceals) us from trouble. We don't have to try to cover ourselves; instead, He is on every side of us, surrounding us from every angle and singing songs of deliverance (escape) from every foe. This is the Creator of the universe we're talking about. You can't get better protection than that! But, we must do our part. We must enter into the secret place, His presence. Psalm 91 says that if we dwell (remain) in the secret place of the Most High we shall abide under the shadow (defense) of the Almighty. So, settle in to His presence and refuse to be moved from your place of rest by anything, anyone, and any circumstance. This rest, the secret place, is your place of protection and victory.

Psalm 32:7 says that God is our hiding place. What does that mean, exactly? It means that He is our protection, covering, secret place and disguise. When we choose to rest in Him, we are undetectable to the enemy; we are in stealth mode, if you will. We completely drop off the devil's radar! Imagine all that can be accomplished in our lives and the lives of others when Satan can't find us! When we enter His presence and drop our "baggage" (our own will and ways of thinking and doing things) at the door, we can operate from the ultimate hiding place—in Christ. What are you waiting for?! In order to access God as our hiding place, we must trust Him. But we must know Him in order to trust Him. You would never agree to let a stranger make major life decisions on your behalf. Jesus completely entrusted Himself to God's care, even in the face of accusations and adversity because He knew God intimately and was able to rest in the knowledge that God was on His side and taking care to perfect everything that concerned Him. Jesus didn't have His own plan or agenda because He trusted God's plan to be the best. When we get to truly know God, it becomes clear that His plan for us is awesome and that we can trust Him completely. In John 14:10, Jesus demonstrates the relationship God wants us to have with Him. Jesus was *in* the Father; this means he was in a fixed position and in a relationship of rest, giving Himself wholly to the Father. Because of His position, when we are in Christ, when we take our place in Him, we can also enter into a fixed position of rest in His presence. From this position God is able to speak clearly to us, and our words and actions line up with Him because they are His! In fact, as we remain in His presence, resting in Him, he performs the works. Now that's something to shout about! When we enter into the rest of God, we rely on Him and He looses His miracle-working dunamis power into our situation.

There is a place designed just for us that the Lord longs to take us to, where we will experience a rest like no other. The place is His presence. Isaiah 11:10 declares that the Root of Jesse, who is Jesus Christ, shall stand as a banner for His people. A standard or banner is something that is set up by authority (in this case, God) to serve as a rallying point where people gather, especially in time of battle. It is also used as a model or example. Jesus has been set up as our Divine Example and the One to whom we are to run in time of battle. The verse goes on to tell us that even the Gentiles (formerly non-believers) will recognize Him and seek after Him in order to come to Him. The word seek doesn't mean to casually look for; instead, it means to diligently inquire, require, pursue, frequent, search or worship. It denotes a continual, habitual seeking, a following after to adhere to His ways. The reward? His rest and His glory.

The world can be a very stressful place. Deadlines, commitments, and obligations are all stressful and even "leisure" pursuits can become downright un-leisurely! Paul knew that stressors faced (and would continue to face) believers when he was writing the letters to the churches. In the book of Philippians, he admonishes believers to "be anxious for nothing" (Phil. 4:6). How can this be possible? According to Webster's Dictionary, the word anxious means to be full of care, to take thought about, to be distracted, divided, and disunited. He knew that the devil would try to bring situations and circumstances to New Testament believers (those who have accepted Jesus Christ as their Lord and Savior) in an attempt to distract, divide and wreak havoc in both the believers individually and in the church as a whole. It's easy to focus on the problem, but that brings no solution and instead makes the anxiety and stress worse. Paul instructs the church to turn away from stress and turn instead to God through prayer and thanksgiving. When we consciously make the effort to focus on Him, spending time praising and thanking Him, letting our thoughts and needs be known to Him, something supernatural happens! It is then that His peace excels over anything our mind or intellect can produce and is able to act as a guard. This peace literally stands watch over us like a sentinel and protects our hearts and minds. How is this accomplished? It is accomplished through Christ Jesus. The word through is the most important part, since it denotes a fixed position (in place, time or state), a relation of rest, and giving oneself wholly to Him. In other words, when we stop in the middle of our mess and focus on Him, entering into the secret place and remaining there in rest, God causes His very own supreme peace to act as a guard over all our thoughts, feelings, and our entire purpose. That's some kind of protection! So enter in today and experience the rest and peace that only come as a result of abiding in Him.

The "weight of the world" is a strategy that the devil uses against us. Have you ever felt like things were just piling up against you and that if something weren't removed you would be crushed under the weight? You are in good company. Paul knew that assignments from the enemy were stacked up against him and he even asked God repeatedly to remove them—after all, Paul was a missionary, doing the work of the Lord. It was then that God revealed His secret to overcoming these burdens—resting in Him. In 2 Corinthians 12:9, God tells Paul that His grace is sufficient for Paul. God goes on to say that His strength (the Greek word *dunamis*—miraculous power, ability, might and abundance) is made perfect (finished, accomplished, full) in weakness. In other words, in the midst of trouble, chaos, stress and upset, we can rest in Him, trusting that His miraculous power will be enough for every situation. Just like in 2 Chronicles 17:20, God specializes in victories when things seem impossible. That's the kind of God we serve!

God's hiding place allows us to separate ourselves from the people and events around us. It can be easy, and even comfortable, to be part of the crowd and to blend in and feel safe. At times, being separated can leave us feeling exposed and vulnerable. But I've found that it is in times of separation that I receive direction, strength and rest. In Mark 7:33, we are told that Jesus took the deaf, mute man aside from the crowd. In other words, He separated him, and talked to him privately. Now I am not suggesting that you cannot receive instruction while others are present, and the corporate anointing often helps us to enter in by charging the atmosphere with expectancy, but there are times and situations when you just can't receive what you need unless you step aside with Him. In this case, the man had to come out from the throng of people and meet with Jesus face to face. The same was true of Moses when God wanted to give him specific instructions or deepen His relationship with him. The Lord is calling us to turn aside from the multitude, to give our full attention to and place our expectation on Him. Then He will pour into us, bringing refreshment, correction, adjustment and strength to us so that we may continue to run our race for Him.

In the time of Zechariah the prophet, the people of God had already suffered much. They were returning from exile in foreign lands and their previous captors had devastated their own lands. Zechariah 10 gives us a picture of what the Lord wants from His people and what He is willing to do on our behalf, even in times which are less than optimal. Zechariah 10:1 tells us to ask the Lord for the rain in the time of the latter rain (spring). This is a time of year when rain seems to be in abundance, no matter what area of the country you live in. Why would we need to ask Him for rain when it is a naturally occurring event at that time? He is requiring us to seek after Him, no matter what things look like in the natural. We must seek Him and ask for His provision rather than assume it is there or depend on what we know or have experienced in the world. When we abide in His presence and seek after Him, He sends abundant provision. In fact, when we do, He promises that we will be redeemed (rescued) and increased (enlarged) (Zech. 10:8). He encourages us, despite circumstances or surroundings, to return to Him and when we do, we enter into His secret place, the place of protection and provision. By coming out from our surroundings and into His presence, our enemies can be vanquished (Zech. 10:11) and we will be preserved and strengthened. In Zechariah 10:12, the Lord promises to strengthen His people in Him (His lordship), allowing us to "walk up and down" in His name. In other words, we access His honor, authority, character, fame, renown, and report because we are hidden in Him. There is no better deal in the universe!

No matter what situation or circumstance you find yourself up against, there is one place the devil can't keep you from being—in His presence. In Acts 16, Paul and Silas were locked up in the inner dungeon of the prison, feet shackled with metal bonds to the floor. It was not humanly possible for them to free themselves, but they knew their Father God well enough to know He had other plans. In the midst of what seemed to be a hopeless situation, they chose to rest in Him, to hide under the shadow of His wings. When they began to praise and worship Him and to lift their voices to exalt the One who is worthy, things changed drastically. Acts 16:26–27 detail that suddenly there was a violent shaking of the foundations of the jail. Everything that their place of bondage was built upon was shifted and moved by the miracle-working power of God. The doors holding them (and everyone else) were opened *immediately* and their chains were loosed. How about that?! Our relationship with God and our refusal to come out of our place of rest and become entangled in the devil's plans not only frees us but helps others to be loosed from their bondage. And the jailer was suddenly awakened. Do you want to see victory in your own life and the anointing to affect change in the lives of others? Don't let Satan move you from your place of rest in God. Focus on His faithfulness, character and promises and proclaim them. You will see mighty victories when this is your battle plan.

Let's look at our divine example, Jesus. Have you ever wondered what the key to Jesus' ministry on earth was? It's true He was God, but here He was all man, living in the flesh like we are, with its noisy appetites and demands. It had to be this way so He could carry our sins and free us from their power to separate us from God eternally. Had He not lived in a mortal body, it would have been a deal-breaker. So, how did He do it? He spent quality time with His Father regularly. Mark 1:35 shows us that He rose early (long before daylight) before the bustle of the day and the demands of people ate up His time, just to get into the presence of God. What did He gain? He gained the very power to complete His mission on earth (and we all have one, you know). He got alone (in a solitary place) with God and prayed. This was the means by which Jesus sustained His spiritual effectiveness. During these times, He was able to shut out everything that competed for His attention and focus entirely on God. He received direction from the Holy Spirit as well as the strength and grace necessary to equip Him for every task. I know that I personally need that. God never gives us an assignment that we can accomplish fully and successfully without His help. Do you want to experience the kind of sustained spiritual effectiveness that Jesus did? Then take note to do what He did—spend time resting in the secret place, talking to and listening to the One who birthed new life in you and called you according to His purpose.

Another thing I've discovered about entering into the hiding place is that not everyone is going to go there. Have you ever wondered why Jesus used parables with the crowds but explained them in detail when asked by His disciples? It boils down to relationship. Not everyone can know you on the same level. There are those who are close, such as immediate family and inner circle of friends, and there are those who are more distant, such as work acquaintances and neighbors. Those closer to us know more details about our lives, opinions, interests, and struggles. In Mark 4:10–11, those who were closest to Jesus, the ones who were there when the big crowds went home, asked Him to explain the parable of the sower to them. It was then that He told them what they wanted to know. Why? It was simply because they had a deeper relationship with Him than the crowd did. These were the ones who dwelt with Him, ate meals with Him, slept near Him, and travelled with Him. He told them that it was given to them to know the mysteries (secrets) of the Kingdom, but that those who were outside (strangers) received all things as parables. How can we know the secret counsel of God today, receiving detailed instruction for life? We can do this by getting close to Him, by spending time reading and praying, and by becoming one of His "inner circle." When we do, all things become clearer as the Holy Spirit imparts wisdom, unveiling Kingdom mysteries to us.

This is why it is so vital to take time to be alone with God and seek His face. Jesus told His disciples (dedicated followers) not only to pray (and this was *not optional,* Matthew 6:6) but also to go to a place where they could be alone with God uninterrupted. He instructed them to "shut the door" to distractions and their own agenda, and to seek God who is in the secret (private) place. It will involve diligence and purposeful effort to locate this place. It will require both time and focused attention to enter into the secret place where God dwells. But oh, the rewards it will bring! When we enter this place we are concealed from the outside world and its stress, problems and attacks. It is not that those things cease to exist; it is just that we are safely hidden by the One who has all the answers! Matthew 6:6 goes on to say that our Father God sees us in the secret place and rewards us *openly!* The word openly means to be apparent, public, manifest, made known, and outward. In other words, not only do we receive protection and peace in the safety of the secret place, but we also receive His provision and everyone can see it. God advertises the benefits of relationship through us. This, in a word, is amazing.

Did you know that there is a place that's inaccessible to the enemy, a place where we are not only untouchable but undetectable to him? Psalm 46:7 declares that the Lord of Hosts is with us and the God of Jacob is our refuge (defense, inaccessible place). In other words, our God is ready and willing to fight for us in the appointed time while hiding us in a place to which the enemy has no access! The word inaccessible denotes without access, unreachable, unable to communicate with, deal with, see, use, or influence. We can enter into this place and dwell there. Psalm 91:1 tells us that he who dwells in the secret place of the Most High shall abide under the shadow of the Almighty. When we do, we will say (declare) of the Lord "He is my refuge (inaccessible place) and our fortress; my God in Him I will trust" (Ps. 91:2). When we are hidden in the secret place of His presence we are able to rest, to be still and to know that He is God (Psalm 46:10), no matter what else is going on around us.

Did you ever build a fort? My brother and I used to take blankets and the couch cushions to construct a fort in the living room. In our minds it was a grand and impenetrable structure, a safe place to hide and to plan. As an adult, I realize how far from the truth this was but I also now know that people continue to build structures of this sort, although not typically out of blankets and couch cushions. When we pursue our own plans, in our own strength and intellect, with our own resources, we build glorified couch forts. Although we may perceive them to be grand and impenetrable, others, including our adversary, the devil, see the foolishness of this belief. There is certainly no couch fort that is able to withstand the storms of life with the wind and waves they bring. But, if the enemy can keep us believing in our false sense of security, disaster will hit unexpectedly and forcefully. As children of God, we have the option of real security and a real hiding place without defect, and it is found in the presence of the Lord. In 2 Samuel 22:2–4, David describes this place. He declares that the Lord is our rock, our fortress and our deliverer. In Him we are to place our trust (flee for protection). David goes on to say that God is our shield and the horn (power) of our salvation, our high tower, our refuge and our savior. God is the One who saves us from violence (wrong, damage). As we call Him and give Him the praise He's for which He's worthy, He shows up and saves us from our enemy. Now that is the type of fort we can trust to keep us safe! Make it your first (and only) choice of hiding, for this alone is the place where the enemy's access to us is denied.

As the world winds down, getting closer to the end of the age, there is a widening cavern between the children of God and unbelievers. In fact, it will become more and more clear who belong to Him and who do not. Times will become more difficult, but our actions in difficulty will clearly demonstrate our allegiance. In short, there will be no middle ground on which to stand. Jeremiah 16:19–21 speaks of such a time and the inevitability of non-believers seeing the difference in those who have made Jesus their Lord. The lordship of Jesus in our lives enables our access to Him as our strength, our fortress and our refuge in the time of affliction (Jer. 16:19). The verse goes on to declare that Gentiles (non-believers) will see this and come to God from all across the world, saying that they have inherited lies, worthlessness (emptiness, dissatisfaction) and unprofitable things because their ancestors have taught them to make gods of things which are not God. This doesn't just pertain to other regions of the world where they worship golden cows, trees, cats or Buddha statues. This has happened right here in America, where we have learned to worship self, money and status symbols. But God tells us in Jeremiah 16:21 that He will cause unbelievers to know His hand and His might. And in this manner, they will understand that His name is the Lord. As we press in to Him and acknowledge all that He is, hiding ourselves in Him, God uses our posture of rest as a sign to the unbeliever, pointing the way to Himself. What an awesome design to lead them to salvation and truth.

Sometimes it feels like there is no safe place to stand where we won't be caught in the shifting sands of public opinion. Where can we go to find safety and refuge, to be strengthened and renewed? God has the perfect place for His children to abide and receive from Him—His secret place. There are, however, some qualifications necessary to enter. In Jeremiah 4, the prophet has just finished calling Israel and Judah to repentance for their idolatrous ways. What is idolatry? It is putting anything or anyone in a position above God in our lives. Even if we have prayed the sinner's prayer, if we fail to make Him Lord and Master of our lives we are not truly His, for we have chosen to put something else (self, money, children, whatever) in His place as our master. In Jeremiah 4:1, Jeremiah instructs those he called to repent to make necessary changes in their lives. First, he says they must return to the Lord. Then, they must put away their abominations. Once they do this, renouncing and removing anything that has taken His place, Jeremiah declares that they shall not be moved. When we choose to serve Him, obeying Him above all other things, we are set in a strong place, one of refuge and support, and can inherit the promises God's provided for us. James 1:6–8 declares that we are to ask without wavering (being moved, double-minded) for if we waver, we receive nothing from the Lord. He wants us to trust Him, enter into rest, and be assured of His care and our victory in Him! James 1:8 goes on to say that a double-minded man is unstable in all his ways. No wonder those who aren't sure of His faithfulness and character feel tossed to and fro, unable to make much headway. It's like a carnival bridge that keeps shifting, moving up and down as they try to navigate across it. It's impossible to get very far and is exhausting! Returning to Him (Jeremiah 4:1) isn't a suggestion but rather an answer. It is a condition that must be met, along with repentance, if we are to be steadfast, without wavering. If we return and put away our abominations, THEN we shall not be moved. The choice is ours. We chose who or what sits on the throne of our lives and there is only room for one. When we choose to swear (take an oath) that the Lord lives in truth, in judgment, and in righteousness then we shall bless ourselves in Him and in Him we will find glory. In this condition, from this place and posture, we are able to reflect His light to the dark and sinful world around us.

Aren't you glad to know that as Christians we have a safe harbor, a place of refuge from the storms of life and from the evil one? But a shelter doesn't do any good unless we run to it and hide ourselves within it. It is like having an umbrella and refusing to open it when the rain comes. You are still getting wet despite being in possession of the umbrella. When we fail to seek His face, when we attempt to figure things out on our own or handle situations in our own strength, we are "getting wet," so to speak. And it is entirely unnecessary! Proverbs 18:10 declares that the name of the Lord is a strong tower, the righteous run to it and are safe. When we encounter storms, difficulty or trouble, we are to run to Him and hide ourselves in His authority and character, so that we are inaccessible to our enemy. By dwelling in His presence, we are in a position of security where our adversary can't touch us! Deuteronomy 33:27 tells us that the eternal God is our refuge and underneath are the everlasting arms (help). It's so good to know that He has a continuing force and power undergirding the dwelling place of safety He's made for us. The verse goes on to say that He will thrust out the enemy and say, "destroy!" We can have complete confidence that when we are abiding in Him, He will take care of our enemies. So, no matter what you are facing today—sickness, confusion, turmoil, lack, adversity—run to the One who has you covered, literally! He will hide you away in an inaccessible place where you can rest and watch Him expel the enemy and utterly destroy it! Glory to God!

The book of Joel, though short, is packed with details about the effects of sin and the coming judgment. It also details the power of God that will be poured out during the end times. In fact, there will be a mighty outpouring of the Spirit of God in those days (Joel 2:28–29). When the world order is falling apart, He promises to be with those who call on Him, and save (rescue) them. God knows who His children are, those who are unwilling to compromise or bow their knee to the demands of the world. Joel 3:16 states that He will be a shelter for His people. He also promises to be the strength of His children—a fortified place, defense, fortress and rock. How can we ensure that we are among those who experience His shelter? Psalm 91 tells us "he who dwells in the secret place of the Most High shall abide under the shadow of the Almighty" (Ps. 91:1). It also says that we will be able to say of the Lord, "He is my refuge and fortress, my God, in Him I will trust" (Ps. 91:2). The word dwell means to sit down, remain, settle, abide and marry. The secret place is a hiding place or covering. To abide means to stay permanently, tarry, and continue. This is not a casual, occasional relationship. You would never consider marrying someone you barely know; you would spend time getting to know them intimately—their dreams, desires, and character. This is the type of relationship in which we can call Him our shelter, refuge, and fortress. As believers, we do not need to fear these last days; rather we must be diligent in seeking Him (Joel 2:12–17), pressing in to release His awesome majesty on our behalf. He promised never to leave or forsake us (Hebrews 13:5). Let us not leave the shelter of abiding in relationship with Him.

I love Psalm 62, especially the description that it gives us of God in verse 7. He is described as our salvation, our glory, the Rock of our strength and our refuge. The utter magnitude of this description blows me away! The Hebrew word for salvation encompasses liberty, deliverance, prosperity, safety, preservation, rescue, defense, and victory. I'm able to experience all of these through my Savior. He is also my glory—splendor, honor and weightiness. He is my strength. Finally, it describes God as my refuge. This means that He is my shelter, hope, trust, protection and confidence. He has our every need covered no matter what the circumstance or trial. First Corinthians 10:13 tells us that in every temptation (test, experience of evil, adversity or trial), He makes us a way of escape so that we are able to bear it. Psalm 32:7 goes on to describe Him as our hiding place, the One who preserves (guards, protects, conceals, and watches over) us, keeping us from trouble. We have to come to know the Lord as these things, to spend time in His Word and prayer, allowing our revelation of Him and His character to invade our consciousness. Only in this manner will we be able to dwell in the secret place, our place of refuge and rest, while chaos and trouble swirl all around us.

Lord, I pray that You would teach me about entering your hiding place, the place where I am inaccessible to the devil and his strategies. Thank You for making it possible for me to come to know You in such an intimate way that I can be hidden inside Your presence and take refuge under Your wings. Forgive me for not always accessing this great blessing You have afforded me and help me to make entering in a priority in my life, in Jesus' name.

Chapter 7
Active Waiting

When we hear the word "wait" most of us have an immediate and somewhat negative reaction. We conjure up images of standing around, aimlessly or passively shuffling, with a roadblock between us and what we need or want. This image, however, is far from what the word means in a Biblical context. In Isaiah 33:2, we see the children of God waiting for Him. The word translated as "wait" actually has the following connotations: to bind together, to twist, to expect, to patiently wait, to tarry. The definition of tarry in the Webster's dictionary includes staying somewhere, lingering in expectation, or abiding. The definition of wait, also as defined in Webster's dictionary, is to remain stationary in readiness or expectation or to look forward expectantly. In contrast to our everyday definition, "waiting" is definitely not aimless or passive. In fact, expectation is attached to this concept. The people in Isaiah were waiting for God but they were also expecting Him to do something for them and to move on their behalf. What were they expecting? They were expecting Him to be gracious (favor) to them. They knew the character of their Father. They also expected God to be their arm (strength) and salvation in the time of trouble. The waiting they were doing was definitely not a casual, aimless waiting and it is the kind of attitude we should aim to have. As His children, we need to adopt the posture of waiting also outlined in Psalm 62:5. It instructs us to wait only upon God, for our expectation (hope) is from Him.

Rest is not the same thing as complacency. The world's view of rest is the absence of activity, but this is not the Lord's view. In fact, He makes a big distinction between the two. In Zephaniah 1:12, the prophet tells us that the Lord will search and punish (judge) the men (and women) who are settled in complacency, who think He is powerless or irrelevant. What does "settled in complacency" mean? The Hebrew word for settled literally means congealed or curdled—like a liquid that has sat for way too long and has turned to something unusable and potentially dangerous. The definition of complacency is to be satisfied with the way things are and not want change. It is marked by self-satisfaction, especially when accompanied by a lack of awareness of actual dangers and deficiencies, and a lack of concern. Like a lobster in a pot of cold water on the stove, the complacent fail to recognize their dangerous position or that the situation is heating up and will bring about their demise!

Frequently, people trust in the world's system, believing that they can do as they please and that somehow the Lord will give them a pass or that their money, position or influence can "get them out of" trouble. This is simply not true. No amount of money can deliver us from the consequences of sin, only a relationship with Jesus, who shed His blood to pay for our sins, can do that. Zephaniah 2:3 gives us instruction on how to avoid judgment in the outpouring of God's wrath (and his wrath is coming more quickly than we know). It tells us to seek the Lord, to humble ourselves, to uphold His justice, and to seek righteousness. This is in direct contrast to complacency. We are also to uphold His justice (decree, divine law, statute). God's Word is Truth and it is not open to interpretation, amendment or changes based on our "evolution as a people." We are to be humble and submit to His authority and rule. Then we will be hidden in the day of the Lord's anger (Zephaniah 2:3). Zephaniah 3:1–2 show us a portrait of people following the world's system, which is in direct opposition to resting in God. We see that God is directly opposed to those who are rebellious and polluted. Who fits this definition? People who have not received correction, who have not obeyed His laws, and who have not trusted Him or drawn near to Him. Resting in Him and abiding in His presence and His Word requires our attention and effort. It is not a position of "going with the flow" (complacency) but rather a position of going with God, which is against the flow. When we choose to go with Him, we can

Active Waiting

settle in because we are hidden in His presence and experience His promises (Zephaniah 3:14–20).

What if you signed up for a team or committee but never bothered to show up for practice, meetings, or games? Would you still be considered part of the team? It is most likely that your name would be dropped from the roster because you did not show up and participate. In fact, I dare say that you would not receive any credit or get to participate in any accomplishments or victories! The same is true in Christianity. In fact, the Bible tells us in John 4:23–24 that those who worship God must do so in spirit and truth, for this is what God is seeking. He is not looking for just a bunch of names to fill His book but rather for people actively participating in His plan not only for redemption but for life! We are to work out our own salvation with fear and trembling (Phil. 2:12). Does this mean we save ourselves by our own works? Absolutely not! It means that we must consciously choose to participate in a relationship with the One Who has already paid the price and won the victory for us! Think of it like taking care of children. As a parent, I am obligated to feed and provide for my own children rather than my neighbor's kids. God is no different! His provision is for *His* children, those in relationship with Him! He is bound by His Word to fulfill the promises He has made to those who are children of faith and those who are made righteous by the blood of the Lamb. In fact, the Word declares in Isaiah 57:21 that there is no peace (safety, prosperity, wholeness) for the wicked. This refers to any of us who are living outside of a relationship with Christ (Rom. 3:23). In fact, we can be in this state and be in the church! In Matthew 7:22–23, Jesus told His followers that on the day of judgment that there would be many who called Him "Lord" that He didn't know.

So what is our directive if we want to remain "on the team" and to have a relationship with Him? We find the answer in John 8, where Jesus tells those who believe "if you abide in My Word, you are My disciples indeed." As we seek Him through His Word, through prayer and through assembling with His body, we abide in Him. It is then that we will know the Truth and the Truth will make us free.

Diligence and rest don't seem to belong together, in a natural sense. When I think about the word diligence, I imagine someone who is hard working and who scurries around until all is completed, and only *then* gets to sit down, relax, and rest. Isaiah 55:8 tells us, however, that our thoughts and ways are not like the Lord's. A prime example of this is found in the area of rest. Hebrews 4:11, Paul encourages us to be diligent in order to enter the rest God has promised. What is Paul talking about? The word diligent used in this verse is translated as making an effort or being prompt or earnest. In other words, we are to on-purpose make the effort to know Him and study His Word so we don't miss His promise of rest. More than anything, God desires good things for us and for all His blessings and promises to be fulfilled in our lives. But we need to do things His way and to abandon our human stubbornness and yield our bodies, our minds, our thoughts and our actions to His leading. This is where grace comes in; it gives us the power to live a life that pleases Him and fulfills His plans and purposes. He not only promises us real rest; He provides the means to accomplish it by His grace. All we need to do is to be diligent in our pursuit of Him. You have to admit that that is a pretty incredible offer.

While we are pursuing the road to peace God's way, the world tries to insert its own slant on it. Politicians and activists seem to be shouting "Peace!" more and more, yet the world appears to be growing darker and more violent as time progresses. The Bible promises that the days will grow darker as the end approaches, with wars and rumors of wars, famines, pestilence and rioting. So how are we, as believers, to live during these troubling and trying times? First Thessalonians 5 tells us that as the world shouts "Peace and safety!" sudden destruction will come upon it (1 Thess. 5:3). But can we, as Christians, experience things differently? In verse 13 of this same book, you will find the answer—we are to be at peace among ourselves. The word "among" is the key here. It means being in a fixed position in time, place or state and giving oneself wholly to something. During the hard things the world as a whole will encounter as the end of the age draws near, believers are able to remain in His peace by diligently practicing and giving ourselves wholly to the rest that is only found in His presence. This is not the manufactured peace birthed from treaties or a police state, but rather the overwhelming quietness and prosperity found in seeking the face of the One who is Himself peace. The saying "no God, no peace; know God, know peace" is true. Until we take the time and expend the energy to know Him intimately and to learn His ways, no amount of striving can bring about the peace we desire.

So what, then, is our part (or role) in waiting and entering into rest? As believers, we are called to do just that—believe. This word means much more than we typically understand. It means to entrust, to commit and to have faith in. We use the word frequently, but to "believe" is not meant to be casual. It suggests both commitment to and reliance upon something, two things that are rare in our age of situational ethics and ever-changing opinion. In much the same way, the word "disciple" means committed learner, pupil or follower. Belief and discipleship require effort on our part—studying the Word, giving time to pray and entering into His presence. These things can't be achieved with casual acquaintance. Oh, but consider the benefits when we purposefully give ourselves to Him and invest in a real relationship with Him! Mark 16:17–18 speaks of the manifestations that will follow those who take the time to truly know Him and place their trust completely in His name (His authority and character). They will move in the power and demonstration of the Lord, cast out demons, speak with new tongues, walk in His protection (against harmful things) and see the sick recover! Why? Because when you truly know Him—His Word, His character, His authority—God is able to work WITH you to confirm (establish) His Word through supernatural, tangible and miraculous signs and wonders. This is beyond incredible!

Jesus commanded His disciples to wait for the Promise of the Father (Acts 1:4). In other words, He wanted His disciples to stay away from the distractions of the world and remain focused on what God had said to them and promised. In other words, they were resting in Him with their expectancy turned up to the fullest! The result? They received power from the Holy Ghost to go out and do all God called them to do to bring His Kingdom purpose to pass. The model has not changed—He is saying the same thing to His disciples today. We are to be actively waiting upon His presence to receive instructions and power to carry those instructions out.

Rest (His rest) is a promise from God. We see in Hebrews 4:1–11 that this promise remains and has not been done away with, therefore it is possible to enter into God's kind of rest no matter what is going on around us. Having said that, it is also entirely possible to fall short of entering His rest. The truth is, even though Jesus already paid the price for our admission ticket to God's rest and it was finished before the foundation of the world, so many of His people have missed out. Although we no longer have to work to accomplish our own peace, we do have to make an effort to enter into His peace. We have to be diligent in order to know the Word of God but for it to be profitable, diligence must be mixed with faith. In other words, we must believe in order to enter (come into) His rest. Second Corinthians 1:20 assures us that *all* the promises of God (healing, peace, rest, joy, victory, prosperity) are "yes" and "amen" in Christ. Let's not fall short by failing to enter into the fullness of any of His promises. We are called to make a diligent effort every day to possess them by faith.

I love the eleventh chapter of Hebrews, the "hall of faith" chapter. It is an awesome account of great who obtained God's wonderful promises, which would have been impossible in the natural, through their faith. As I was reading and pondering on it, I realized that there is a "rest" of faith. The Greek word for faith describes belief, reliance upon assurance, constancy and conviction. These very components are integral to rest. In order to enter into rest, we must believe that God is (that he exists) and that He rewards those who diligently seek Him (Heb. 11:6). This is exactly the method by which we enter into the secret place—the place of His rest. Therefore, it seems that the more we enter into His presence in the secret place, the more our faith grows and the more we are able to abide in God's rest. Why? Because we become so intimately acquainted with God, His character, personality and power, that we are able, like Abraham, Enoch and the other "Fathers of Faith," to settle down in His promises and be completely confident in the knowledge that He is working on our behalf and will accomplish His purpose and plan for our lives. What is our job in this wondrous process? Our job is to activate our faith by making the words we speak and the thoughts we think line up with Truth—His Word. So, go ahead and enter into the "rest of faith" and trust that God is both willing and able!

In order to be active in our resting, we must be connected to the Source of power. Just as a natural plant can't bear any fruit if it is separated from its source of supply (the roots, going into the earth where they receive nutrients and nourishment, which enable them to reproduce), neither can we bear fruit when we are separated from God. Separation from God does not just refer to the time before we were saved. Even after we have given our lives to Christ, if we remain aloof, at a distance and doing our "own thing," we will be disconnected from our very source of life and power. The greater the distance from our source, the more difficult it is to receive nourishment. No plant would bloom if we only stuck it in dirt once or twice a week for a few hours or offered it a few drops of water, yet many people relate to God this way and wonder why they feel weak and don't bring forth fruit. Unless we stay in His presence, we cannot carry and bring forth fruit (John 15:5). In fact, the Bible plainly tells us that we can do *nothing!* But, the promise made to us is that if we abide in Him, not only will our fruit be abundant, but our harvest will also be frequent. Making sure that we stay closely rooted in the Source of all life is our job. Our harvest depends on it!

Many think that the Holy Spirit would never ask us to do something difficult or uncomfortable to our flesh. This is simply not true. In Luke 4:1, we see the Holy Spirit leading Jesus into the wilderness to be tempted and to fast for 40 days. This certainly doesn't sound like a good time. The wording in this verse makes it clear, however, that Jesus was full of the Spirit, and that it was the Holy Spirit who led Jesus into the wilderness. Sometimes it is necessary to go through things that cause our flesh to balk because they are uncomfortable or inconvenient. Our physical bodies and minds never want to do what is difficult or painful, but often this is the only way to achieve growth. We would rather sleep than study, but it's in studying that we learn and increase our wisdom and understanding. When we listen to and obey the Spirit of God, He leads us exactly where we need to go to fulfill the next step in His plan and call for our lives. We need to press in and dwell with Him, making Him our place of rest and refreshment so that we are able to complete the next step of our journey. It was the Holy Spirit who sustained Jesus in the wilderness, assisting Him and enabling Him to defeat the devil. The reward for this? Jesus returned from the wilderness in the power of the Spirit to His hometown and began the ministry God had called Him to do, displaying the power and glory of God in everything He did. So the next time you feel the Lord leading you to do something that seems uncomfortable or difficult for your flesh, rest assured that He will not only equip you, He will sustain you and cause you to come out on the other side strengthened and full of His wonder-working power.

There are so many things that compete for our attention and so many roads that beckon to us that the way can seem crowded and confusing. How can we make sure that we are on the right path? God desires to show us the way and He will speak with us along the way about the things to come and what we must do. Isaiah 45:11 and 45:13 speak of this. God says that we are to ask Him about things to come concerning His sons (those in relationship, servants). He is willing to show us and he even requires us to ask Him about the details of our lives because we are in relationship with Him. He's not a God who wants to leave us in the dark but rather He wants to light the way and make it clear. Isaiah 45:11 goes on to say that we are "to command me (God) concerning the work of My hands." In other words, He longs for us to ask diligently about the situations, circumstances, actions and happenings that occur in our lives. God has a plan and purpose for each of us to fulfill and He wants to help us on the way. He doesn't like to see His covenant children stumbling along blindly, taking wrong turns and falling into holes. He's provided light for our path, so it just seems silly that we wouldn't use it to illuminate our journey and make the way easier and safer. Isaiah 45:13 declares that He has raised us up in righteousness and that He will direct our ways. Why would we want to go through life any other way than with His guidance and assistance? The Bible declares that His Word is a lamp to our feet and a light to our path (Ps. 119:105). When we spend time seeking after Him and studying His Word, He reveals the path clearly before us, directing our steps into success (Prov. 3:5–6) without struggling or worrying about missteps.

Daniel is an excellent example of one who actively waited. Daniel was an eyewitness to much devastation and upheaval. His nation was overrun, people were taken from their homes and families were enslaved in a foreign land under an ungodly dictator, pressured to relinquish their faith and follow the dictates of the heathen society. If ever there was a time to cry "foul" and to rage against God and the seeming injustice that His people encountered, Daniel's era would seem to be it. Just where was the God of Israel while His very own people were being abused?

Rather than turning his back on God, Daniel set himself to seek God and to inquire of Him. Daniel, in the midst of turmoil and frustration, set aside his own wants and desires (he fasted all meat, sweets and strong drink) so that he could effectively seek out the only One who could help him and his people. And he repented. Not only for his own sins, but for the sins of his nation, Israel. Now, with all we know about Daniel, he didn't seem much like the rebellious, sinful type. He had already been thrown in the lions' den for choosing to serve God over the commandments of men. But Daniel sought God with his whole being and like other prophets (Isaiah, Jeremiah, and Hosea, to name a few) this seeking led him to encounter the Holy God, making his deeds unmistakably paltry in comparison. In fact, not only did his strength fail at his encounter, but all the men who were with him became terrified and fled, even though they did not see the vision, but only encountered His presence (Dan. 10:18–19) In the presence of God, Daniel encountered an angel with this message: "oh man greatly beloved, fear not! Peace (safety, well being, health, victory, prosperity, favor, rest, wholeness) be to you; be strong, yes be strong!" Just take a look at what happens when we encounter the presence of God. No wonder the devil tries so hard to keep us from Him! Dwelling in His presence, seeking his face and prayer (including repentance) was Daniel's *lifestyle.* It wasn't a once in a while thing, but a daily seeking, a desire to enter into the secret place and fellowship with Almighty God. Why? Because Daniel knew that all he and his nation faced could never be overcome with mere human strength or intelligence. So, when situations, circumstances, and even public policy seem insurmountable, hide yourself in Him, seek His wisdom, and follow His ways. In resting in Him, you will be strengthened.

Submission on our part is critical to a lifestyle of active waiting. We must choose to submit our will, our opinions, and our way of doing things and trust that God knows what we need better than we do. It's essential to our success that we choose to have Him make the calls in our lives. In fact, the Holy Spirit acts much like an umpire. In baseball, the umpire's role is crucial. He calls all the plays. It is the umpire who decides if a pitch is a ball or a strike, if someone is safe or out on base. Without him, there would be chaos. Colossians 3:15 tells us to let God's peace rule (be the umpire, govern, prevail) in our hearts. It also goes on to tell us to be thankful. It must be our conscious decision to allow God's peace to be the decision-making force in our life. As we spend time in His Word and actively submit our lives to Him, the Holy Spirit can lead and guide us in His peace. What a relief it is to allow Him to call all the plays. It certainly takes the pressure off of us! Rest assured that God knows a foul when He sees it and will deal with it accordingly. Playing by His rules decreases chaos and upset in our lives and allows us to focus on being grateful for all He has done for us in Christ. That is truly living!

The benefits of actively entering in to His rest and peace are overwhelming. Who doesn't desire the God of love and peace to be with us as we go through this life? In 2 Corinthians 13:11, Paul talks to the Corinthian believers, bringing correction and encouragement to them. He urges them to become complete. While this can be translated as perfect, the actual meaning does not mean without mistakes. Instead, the Greek word speaks of improving, adjusting, training, disciplining, and making the necessary adjustments and repairs. Just as a torn net cannot catch fish, so a life that does not line up with His word and His will cannot experience the authentic lasting joy and peace He so longs to give to us. In this world of ever-changing morals and values, which is growing darker by the moment, how can we know what needs to be adjusted? God's Word never changes. It is an infallible truth that we can hold our lives up against as a plumb line, allowing us to see where correction and re-alignment are needed. God doesn't give us His Word to scold us or make us feel like failures, but rather to allow us to call upon the name of Jesus and experience the grace we need to become more like Him! Without Him, we can do nothing; but by Him we can run through a troop (divide an army) and leap over a wall. When we spend time with Him, He equips us to live a life pleasing to Him, one of peace, love (the God-kind of love), unity and comfort.

I don't know many people who don't want to enjoy or even love life. In fact, I've never overheard an individual stating that he/she wishes life was harder or less enjoyable. On the contrary, I've frequently heard comments that people in general desire a more fun-filled or easier life, one with fewer obstacles and trials and more joy. The first epistle of Peter gives us a glimpse of one of the keys to obtain get this coveted prize. In 1 Peter 3:10–12, Peter states that anyone looking for a life he/she loves and wanting to see good days has a list of things to do that will contribute to this end. Included on this list are: refraining from speaking evil and lying; turning away from doing evil/sinful things; doing good; and, finally, seeking peace and pursuing it. This last point is the one I want to highlight. We are to seek peace, which can only come from God. Not only are we to require peace, we are to pursue it. In order to pursue something, we must follow after it, press forward and strive to attain it!

Sounds like something that takes effort, not something that happens automatically, doesn't it?! This is what is meant by striving to enter into His rest. We must purposefully spend time with God, reading His Word, praying and talking to him, and listening to His voice, all while praising and thanking Him for His goodness. Do you want to love life and see good days? Then it is time to start desiring and requiring His peace, making the effort necessary to enter into it.

It seems like a given that one must stand before they can walk. We take it for granted because we see it in normal child development. However, when it comes to our Christian walk, we seem to forget this. In Galatians 5:1, Paul instructs the believers at Galatia to "stand fast" in their liberty. Standing, like rest, is not a passive thing, but rather an active posture. It requires something of the person standing. When children first learn to stand, it requires much effort to maintain the upright posture against the effects of gravity. Why? Because muscles are weak, balance is impaired and the posture is largely unfamiliar. As the child spends more time practicing standing, strength and balance improve and the upright position becomes second nature. Why then, would we not need to practice standing (abiding) in the Spirit? How can we possibly move forward successfully in the call and purpose of God when we don't spend time in His presence, practice resting in Him, listen to His voice or obey His commands? It would seem silly for us to expect a newborn to stand and walk yet we don't consider taking time to abide in Him essential to the Christian walk. This is where we are mistaken! If we desire to walk in the Spirit successfully, we must begin with rest, which will enable us to stand! From there we are able to walk (live, follow after) in the Spirit, and we won't fulfill the lust of the flesh (Galatians 5:16). If we hope to successfully complete the plan and purpose of God in our lives, we must free ourselves from the yoke of sin that Jesus already paid the price for, and learn to abide (remain) in the Spirit, living and following after His leading and guidance. The more we practice being in His presence, the more skilled we will become.

There are benefits to cultivating a deep, intimate, abiding relationship with the Lord. In the book of Acts, we see time and again people who were pressing into Him, seeking His face, and we see how He responded to them. Cornelius (Acts 10) was a man who prayed, fasted and gave. His relationship with God got him noticed by God (much the same as Job). Because of the depth of this relationship, God gave him explicit, detailed instructions about whom he needed (Peter) and where to find him (Simon's house in Joppa, by the sea). God not only honored Cornelius' relationship with Him, but also Peter's. He was able to give Peter the green light to go with the Gentiles (strictly forbidden) to Cornelius' house to meet his need. In fact, the Holy Ghost told Peter to go without doubting. Later, when Peter had to explain to his fellow Jewish believers, he was so sure of himself because he knew without a doubt that he had heard from

God (Acts 11:17). It is no surprise that in Philippians 2:5 we are instructed to "let this mind be in you which also was in Christ Jesus." This way we are hooked up to God's thought and plans. His thoughts are not our thoughts nor His ways our ways (Isa. 55:8). When we abandon our way of thinking and doing and rest in Him, He always gives us the plans that lead to success.

Another prime example of someone who knew that waiting required action was the woman with the issue of blood (Luke 8:43–48). Have you ever wondered how Jesus knew that the woman had touched Him? Imagine a huge crowd, with people pushing and shoving, pressing in to get a glimpse of the Master. I'm sure many people "touched" Him, so what made this woman different? The word "touched" doesn't just mean to brush against or have contact with; it means to be attached to. This woman's faith caused her to take action—to become attached to Jesus, to expect Him to make a change in her life. Because she placed a demand on the anointing, His miracle-working power (*dunamis*) was able to flow into her life and change it forever. She realized what few do—that it's not enough to have casual contact in a crowd with Jesus, not enough to say you were there. We have to purposefully attach to Him and seek His face; for it is then that He is able to impart all we need in life to us.

The lame man in Acts 3 also needed something. In order to receive what he needed (his healing), it required him to pay attention to Peter and John, who had been in the

Active Waiting

presence of Jesus and knew their authority in Christ. It also required expectancy. The Bible tells us that through faith in His name the lame man was made whole (Acts 3:16). When he was persuaded and fully believed in the character and authority of Jesus and that Jesus was not only willing but able to heal him, he remained in a state of expectation that healing would occur and he received his miracle. He had entered a state of rest, no longer relying on anything he himself could do, and looked to God to perform what only He could do. Rest is not passive and apathetic, but rather a state of readiness, of expectation and of absolute conviction that God will do what He said He would do. It requires active waiting that is faith engaged and accompanied by complete trust in His character and ability. This, in turn, requires that we spend time with Him, letting Him reveal Himself, His promises and His plan to us.

As you can see, in the Bible, those who had an encounter with Jesus knew it! They begged Him just to let them touch the hem of His robe (Matt. 14:36). When we purpose in our hearts to seek an encounter with Him, we come into contact with His garment, which the Word tells us is His glory and splendor. When we do, we can't help but be transformed. Everyone who touched His garment was made perfectly whole. In other words, they were saved thoroughly, cured, healed, delivered, and protected. He's waiting for us to reach out and touch Him and we do this by getting to know Him. How do you get to truly know something (or someone)?

Studying is the key—taking the time to pay attention, focus on and immerse yourself in the subject. A teacher knows which students have spent time learning the assigned material and which ones have only given a brief review (if any at all). When test time arrives, those who know the subject will shine, without stress or hesitation. It will be easy for them to answer because they are well-acquainted with the subject. The Word of God instructs us to have the mind of Christ (Phil. 2:5) and to study to show that we can rightly divide (dissect) the word of Truth (2 Tim. 2:15). As we spend time in the Word and in the presence of God, we come to know His character and nature intimately and we learn how He thinks and acts. We learn to trust Him fully and rest in His truth. The "tests" that come against us don't seem as hard, because we know the Answers and He never changes. No need to worry or sweat—He is all we need and He is able.

As the world winds down, getting closer to the end of the age, there is a widening cavern between the children of God and unbelievers. In fact, it will become more and more clear who are His and who are not. Times will become more difficult, but our actions in difficulty will clearly demonstrate our allegiance. In short, there will be no middle ground to stand on. Jeremiah 16:19–21 speaks of such a time and the inevitability of non-believers seeing the difference in those who have made Jesus their Lord. The lordship of Jesus in our lives enables our access to Him as our strength, our fortress and our refuge (escape) in the time of affliction (trouble, adversity) (Jer. 16:19). The verse goes on to declare that Gentiles (non-believers) will see this and come to God from all across the world, saying that they have inherited lies, worthlessness and unprofitable things because their ancestors have taught them to make gods of things which are not God. This doesn't just pertain to other regions of the world where they worship golden cows, trees, cats or Buddha statues. This pertains to us right here in America, where we have learned to worship self, money and status symbols. But God tells us in Jeremiah 16:21 that He will cause unbelievers to know His hand (power, ability) and His might. And in this manner, they will understand that His name is the Lord! As we press in to Him and acknowledge all that He is, hiding ourselves in Him, God uses our posture of rest as a sign to the unbeliever, pointing the way to Himself. What an awesome design to lead them to salvation and truth.

It seems like the world wants to push us into a defensive state, demanding an account of our beliefs and bullying us into submitting to its viewpoints. While I am convinced that we must be able to verbalize the reasons for our faith in a manner that is both accurate and compelling, we are not to be intimidated by aggressive unbelief. Someone can disbelieve the law of gravity, however the fact (and effects) of gravity on the earth still remains. I love the account of faith and civil disobedience found in Daniel 3. Shadrach, Meshach, and Abed-Nego we called before King Nebuchadnezzar for their refusal to bow down upon command to the golden idol he had erected. They knew that it could well cost them their lives, for the law stated that anyone who refused to bow would be thrown into the furnace. When questioned the responded with the utmost respect and courtesy while standing up for what (Who) they believed. They never wavered in their faith and told the king that there was no need to defend themselves, stating "we have no need to answer you in this matter." They firmly believed that God would deliver them from both the furnace and the king's hand but maintained that even if they perished, they were unwilling to compromise their beliefs and succumb to the king's ungodly demands. This is the posture we must assume as Disciples of Christ in this hour. As expected, King Nebuchadnezzar was infuriated by their refusal to be "politically correct" and had them thrown into the fire as an example. Despite his best efforts to extinguish their resistance, the king was astonished (shocked) at what he saw. Rather than being consumed by the fire, they were loosed in it, without any harm or damage. In fact, all the government officials saw the men on whose bodies the fire had no power, whose clothing was not even affected! When we take a stand for God and His Truth, even our adversaries will have to admit that our God delivers His servants who trust Him. The unflinching faith we find as we rest in His presence and the knowledge of His Word and character, yielding our bodies to His service, enables us to frustrate the ungodly commands of the government (Dan. 3:28). As we do, it will become abundantly clear that there is no other God who can deliver like our God (Dan 3:29).

Lord, I pray that you teach and train me in the methods of active waiting. Forgive me for the times that apathy and weariness have de-activated my faith, and caused me to miss entering into Your place of rest. Help me to keep my focus on You, regardless of what is going on around me and actively attach myself to You for You are the source of everything I need.

Chapter 8
Restoration

I don't think it's any coincidence that the word restore contains the word rest. Restore, by definition, means to bring back or put back into an original condition by repairing or cleaning. Isn't that just what the Lord does when we learn to rest in Him? When we learn to dwell in His presence, the secret place, we find peace, joy, protection and every provision we need. We are restored to the type of relationship that Adam and Eve enjoyed with God before the fall. When we learn to take time to rest in Him, we can watch Him bring restoration to every area of our lives.

Rest is an integral part of restoration. When we enter into His rest and allow ourselves to experience His peace and stillness, we can then see His salvation (2 Chron. 20:17). The word salvation in the Hebrew is *yshuwah* (Jesus), which is translated as deliverance, victory, prosperity, health, help and aid. That sounds like restoration to me. As we learn to enter into His rest, Jesus shows up to provide all we need, bringing complete restoration in every area—nothing missing, nothing lacking and nothing broken. This is what God desires for all of His children, but sadly, many miss what He is freely offering because they don't enter in to receive it. Psalm 24 declares that the "earth is the Lord's and all its fullness (all that is), the world and all those who dwell therein." He is clearly the One who founded it and established it. The psalm then gives detailed information about who can ascend to the hill and stand in His holy place. This person, a believer, must have clean (innocent) hands and a pure heart. In other words, the ones who can come into His presence and experience His glory must repent, humbling themselves under His hand and be washed clean by the blood of the Lamb. There is no room to enter His gates with arrogance, pride or sinfulness. The believer who is allowed to enter His presence must be one who has not lifted up his soul to an idol (useless thing, destructive evil) or sworn deceitfully (Ps. 24:3–4). When we rid ourselves of every weight of sin by repentance and by the Blood, then we are able to boldly come, seeking Him and receiving blessing and righteousness from the God of our salvation (Ps. 24:5).

When we learn to enter into His rest, God can access all the areas of our life that need restoration. When we are resting, we are free from stress and anxiety and aren't injured by the restoration process, no matter how "deep" God needs to go to repair things or despite what He needs to "cut off." It is a time of refreshment, something to counteract the stress and effects of the harried world we live in. There are those who spend their whole lives attempting to discover rest and pleasure in money, fame, physical relationships, false religions, and the serving of self. The book of Jeremiah tells of a time not dissimilar to our own when people were given to serving all kinds of things rather than the One true God. They piled up rituals and idols in their lives in an attempt to find something that would bring peace and comfort. In Jeremiah 8:15, we see them looking for peace but no good came. In their aimless searching, they looked for a time of health but instead found only trouble. Why do you suppose that people who were obviously being diligent in their pursuit of health and peace came up empty-handed? Because although they were diligent, it was in the wrong direction! Instead of spending their time, energy and resources getting closer to their God, the Author of peace and health, they followed deception, searching for well-being in sources that could never produce it. The Word of God tells us that times of refreshment come from the presence of the Lord. How are we able to access this amazing refreshing and restoration? We are able to do so by repenting and being converted back to whom God created us to be before sin entered the world (Acts 3:19).

We were created to be in continual fellowship and communion with our Creator, the Holy One of Israel. We can't do this while holding on to our own idols, for He is jealous (Deut.

6:15, Nah. 1:2, Zech. 8:2, 2 Cor. 11:2) and won't share our affection with anyone or anything else. If you want to experience His peace and have him refresh your life, lay down everything that takes your focus off of Him and anything that competes for your time and affection. When you do, His presence will flood over you, bringing a fresh and proper perspective, along with new strength and the ability to conquer the tasks that face you.

Learning to rest is about taking God at His Word and trusting Him with everything you have and everything you are. When you spend time getting to really know Him, you will truly "taste and see that the Lord is good" (Ps. 34:8). When you begin to discover all that He is it is no longer a struggle to trust Him or to lie down and rest in His faithfulness and His complete ability to manage every situation perfectly, even without your "two cents." Sometimes, however, we hold back, despite what we have read, seen and experienced about God. Everyone is looking for a sure thing, someone or something that won't let them down. Unfortunately, it is exceedingly rare to find. Call it advertising, but most things are not as they appear; they give an illusion of a trustworthiness that is all too often false. This undermines our confidence and leaves us disillusioned and skeptical. It can also lead to depression and even hopelessness. Our position as children of God leaves us in a different place, however. We have the opportunity to really know the One who never changes, the one who is the only "real deal."

Isaiah 45 alludes to this. In verse 19, God shows us that He does not speak in secret in a dark place on earth. He also does not call us to seek Him in vain. Instead He speaks righteousness (justice) and declares things that are right. He shines His light of truth into every dark and worthless circumstance and leads us out! This happens when we seek Him and press in to inquire and require Him with all that we are. He promises to save us when we look to Him (Isa. 19:22). In fact, God proclaims that in Him all the descendants of Israel (His disciples) shall be justified and we will have glory (19:25). What a far cry from the empty promises of the world. God can back up His promises because He never changes (Mal. 3:6). We can safely search for Him and put our trust in His character and integrity, without ever suffering disappointment, for He is faithful (Heb. 10:23).

The Word of God tells us that those who choose to die to themselves and be hidden in Christ are blessed and are to be envied, for they obtain rest—a cessation from toil, a refreshment—from their toils, pains, troubles and weariness and none of their works or efforts are wasted (Rev. 14:13 AMP). When we find our rest in Him, He not only removes our struggle and weariness but also prospers what we set our hands to do. This is an awesome promise for those who abide in the secret place. This secret place is found in His presence and allows us to experience His peace. Did you realize before now that there is a perfect peace and that you can enter into the perfect rest of God, despite what's going on around you? Isaiah 26:3 declares that God will keep us in perfect peace ("shalom shalom"). The fact that the words "perfect" and "peace" are the same Hebrew word (shalom) means that this is emphasized. He will emphasize and fulfill our peace. How do we partake of this peace? We must keep our mind stayed on Him. This is not a casual thing, but a full dependence, allowing Him to prop us up with His strength. This is made possible when we trust in Him. We must know Him so intimately that we can trust Him completely; above everything else we see, feel, hear and encounter. It takes time to build such a relationship and effort to maintain it. Oh, but the rewards of knowing Him! The people who know their God shall be strong and do exploits (Dan. 11:32b).

As you can see, true rest is found in His presence. While we can experience rest, peace and refreshment occasionally, true, deep and complete rest comes from staying in His presence *permanently* (Ps, 91:1). Is this possible? God would not have said so if it were not! We need to stop and acknowledge His presence on purpose and practice entering in and continuing to be aware of Him even during our day-to-day activities. When we do this, we will find ourselves surrounded by the protection and provision that no foe can withstand. Times of refreshment and restoration in His presence are *priceless!* And the best part? He not only longs for us, but enables us to enter in to the secret place and experience true fellowship with the only true God, the Creator and Master.

All we need to do is dive in and taste and see that He is good. What are you waiting for?

> "Your part is simply to rest. His part is to sustain you, and He cannot fail."
> —Hannah Whitall Smith

During the time of the prophet Haggai, the nation of Israel had a problem. The exiles were returning to their homeland, which had been destroyed during the Babylonian captivity. Not only were their homes and land destroyed, but the Temple, once magnificent, lay in ruins. Apparently, while in "rebuilding mode" they became somewhat overwhelmed as well as distracted. The task of rebuilding the Temple was daunting and slow; some had seen the former Temple in all its glory and doubted that anything could ever compare. The progress to build homes was moving much more quickly and satisfyingly so the focused their attention there. Apathy regarding the temple set in as opposition to building the temple mounted and finally construction ceased. Have you ever felt so worn out and discouraged that you just gave up? So incapable and unworthy of the task God called you to that you decided to focus on fighting something in your own strength? That is where the people were during Haggai's time. It's easy to get there if you don't spend time abiding in the Lord. The struggles and opposition of the world have a way of sapping our strength and causing us to get our eyes off of Him and onto ourselves. Instead of seeking His will and direction, we seek to comfort and ease the pain of our flesh. This is a losing battle. Whenever we take our focus off what God is doing and focus on self, we step out from the protection of the secret place and into the line of fire. Now the enemy can locate us and the hits just keep coming. Rather than soothing our flesh, we encounter more pain and more problems until we are beaten down. The answer? Focus on Him, trust in Him, and abide in His Word and His presence. He is the guidance we need and He will instruct and strengthen us. He will declare to us that the glory of the latter house shall be greater than that of the former. He will declare that when we set ourselves to seek Him and do His will, it will be in the place where He gives peace (wholeness, prosperity, happiness, health, safety, favor) (Hag. 2:9). When all nations are being shaken, the only place to find rest is in His presence (Hag. 2:7).

How are we to maintain an attitude and atmosphere of peace when trouble is all around us? Is it possible to rest in the midst of the storm? Daniel was faced with severe circumstances more than once. He lived his adult life as a captive in a foreign land. He suffered persecution from others around him because of his faith in God. His nationality and religious beliefs set him apart and caused others to plot against him, frequently because God showed up to help him. No matter the situation, however, it seemed like Daniel overcame it. Why? Because he made rest his habit.

Daniel had unwavering faith, trusting that God would show up on his behalf. In Daniel 6:10 we see a portrait of this trust. It says that Daniel knew that King Darius had been convinced to sign the writing (law, decree) so Daniel went home and prayed. In fact, he prayed three times a day with his windows open, just as he always had. He didn't change a thing, despite what the new law said. Daniel practiced civil disobedience because going along with the new law meant going against what God had commanded. This is the only acceptable reason for believers to disregard the law. This passage shows Daniel in a state of rest. He didn't go home and cry, scream, or call his friends to commiserate about the unjust situation they were in or about the ungodly leadership of Babylon. He also didn't stop openly fellowshipping with his God. In fact, he did things the way he always had, as was his custom and habit. He knew well that it could cost him his life. But, living a life of compromise was not living, for it would mean turning his back on God to follow the dictates of men. Because of his close relationship with God, this was something Daniel simply couldn't do. Instead, he placed his trust in the only One who could deliver him from the mouths of the lions and rested peacefully in His faithfulness. The end result? Despite being thrown into a pit with lions as punishment for breaking the civil law, Daniel not only survived but God also demonstrated His power and lordship to all, even those who were his adversaries. They recognized that because Daniel continually served his God, God delivered him. In our current times of ungodly legislation and moral shipwreck, we need to take our cue from Daniel. It is time to rest in our God, in His faithfulness to protect and deliver His disciples no matter the situation. And He will do it in front of our adversaries, for all the world to see, when we are committed and immovable in standing for our faith. Rest in Him, for He is faithful and just.

Hebrews 13:20–21 speaks of the Lord as the God of peace. This is no quiet, wimpy version of peace mind you, for as soon as the verse speaks of peace, it goes on to identify our God as the same one whose power raised Jesus from the dead. I'd say that His character and authority, and therefore His peace, is pretty powerful! As you allow Him to work in your life through the blood of Jesus, He will surely make you complete in every good work (Heb. 13:21). In other words, by resting in Him and allowing Him to do what only He can do, He equips us for service and success. No amount of worry or striving could ever do that. So today, enter into His presence and rest quietly while He accomplishes the amazing work of His grace and peace in your life.

So how are we to successfully run our race here on earth? The Bible tells us in Philippians 2:5 that we are to have the mind of Christ. We are to entertain the same thoughts, have the same sentiments, set our affection on the same things and share the same opinions as Jesus Himself. Is this possible? Can we really share the same mindset as Christ? Absolutely! But how? We do this when we immerse ourselves in His Word, getting to know His thoughts and actions. When we study what He said and how He did things, we become more like Him. Have you heard it said that old married couples tend to resemble each other? Why do you think that is? Very simply, it is due to the fact that they have spent so much time together. If we want to have the mind and mindset of Jesus, we need to get to know Him intimately, not just casually. When we do we will truly be His representatives on earth in a dark and hopeless world.

The book of Isaiah speaks of a "remnant" of God's people, those who, despite pressures and circumstances all around, return to the Lord and His ways. We see in Isaiah 10:27 that when He returns, the Lord will come against and move the enemies (Assyria) who oppress His remnant people. In fact, He says that their burden will be removed and the yoke (maltreatment, pain, abuse) taken away. Why? The yoke is destroyed because of the anointing. The anointing represents the glory and the presence of the Lord. How can we experience freedom and rest from burdens, pain, abuse and stress? We can do this by returning to Him and running into the secret place, His presence! In Matthew 11:28–30, Jesus tells us the same thing. He instructs those who labor and are heavy laden (overburdened) to come to Him and He will give them rest. By doing so, we willingly exchanging the yoke of the world for His yoke. A yoke can therefore represent bondage (to the world) or benefit (when we link up with Jesus). When we align and balance our lives around

Christ and His character and methods of doing things, stress and work come off of us and we are able to function optimally. How? Because He is meek (gentle, humble) and lowly, His yoke is easy and His burden is light. When we enter into true covenant with Him, yoking together with Him, our stress and burdens are lifted because we allow Him to lead and work in our situations. No longer must we struggle under the weight of things we were never meant to bear. We must consciously decide to allow Him to lift the world's burdens from us and hook up with Jesus today. As you enter His presence, you enter into partnership with Him and rest is inevitable! Separation from the world's system and beliefs is part of Kingdom life, and it is the key to being able to enter into His rest. We do not need to becomes hermits or move to a deserted island, for that would not serve His Kingdom purpose, which is to draw others to Jesus so that they can be saved and enjoy a life lived in Him. Instead, we need to purge all of the things that the world has deposited in us and allow a perfect cleansing so that we can be used effectively. Matthew 3:12 speaks of Jesus winnowing the wheat, which means gathering the wheat while discarding the chaff. This process involves the removal of the outer, undesirable and unwanted coverings of grain and getting rid of them. When we are determined to come close to God and to rest in Him, we trust Him to complete this process in our lives. We are giving Him the authority to remove all the undesirable, useless and inferior things that have crept into us and caused us to experience less than His perfect will for us. These inferior elements not only separate us from our ultimate purpose, but from the One who called us to that purpose. Instead, we need to submit to Him, crawl up into His lap and say "let the wind of Your Spirit blow on me, separating all the dirt and waste matter" so that we can experience true freedom and restoration in our lives by making our home in Him.

Zerubbabel was the governor of Judah at the time when the Temple was to be rebuilt. It was a daunting task and one that would likely take much time, effort, manpower and money. Think of it—the exiles had just returned to their land after it had been pillaged and burned. Rebuilding and restoring the Temple to its former glory seemed incomprehensible. The Lord sent a message to the people through the prophet Zechariah. He told them that they could stop worrying about the "how" because rebuilding was not going to be accomplished through man's might or power. Instead, the Lord declared that the task would be accomplished by His Spirit. In other words, the Lord would empower the people to perform what needed to be done through the rebuilding power by His Spirit. He would give grace to His people as they worked. No matter what task is before you, this empowerment is available to you. If He has called you to something, He promises to make up the difference, to put His "super" on our natural as we rest in Him and do what He's called us to do. In 2 Samuel 22:33, David proclaims that God is his strength and his power, and that He makes his way perfect.

This is a portrait of a man whose life was hidden in his God. David rested in God's ability and was able to accomplish feats of might and valor because he knew his Lord intimately.

I have found that no matter the situation that comes against us, there is a place of rest and protection in the Lord. When we run to Him, seeking comfort and solace, He is there to provide us with that and so much more. In fact, it is in such times that He strengthens us and teaches us to depend upon Him. In Jeremiah 31, we find the Lord working on behalf of His faithful children, the remnant that did not give themselves over to the dictates of the culture around them. They had been taken captive but remained true to Him. Jeremiah 31:2 states that the people who survived the sword found grace (favor, empowerment) in the wilderness. It seems that because they remained faithful to God despite their troubles and in the midst of unfavorable circumstances and chose to trust Him, they were able to rest during the time of drought and "sharpness." And, it continues on to say that the Lord Himself went to give them rest. It is because of His everlasting love for us that He draws us with loving kindness (Jer. 31:3). When we respond to this drawing by diligently seeking Him, turning our focus and attention on Him rather than on whatever circumstance we may find ourselves in, we enter into His presence and find rest and strength.

Our God is such a loving Father. His character, goodness, love, patience, and faithfulness are on display throughout both the Old and New Testaments. We can rest in Him, completely trusting that when we rely on Him, He will take care of us. Even when we cause our own problems or hurt, when we repent and cry out to Him, He is faithful and will come and rescue us. Psalm 107 tells of the many things we become ensnared in as well as His unending willingness to take us back when we turn from our rebellion against His rightful Lordship and authority. When we cry out to the Lord in our trouble, He saves us from our distresses. But He doesn't stop there. He sent His word to heal us and delivers us from all of our destructions (pitfalls) (Ps. 107:19–20). Humbling ourselves, repenting and drawing near are the best things we can do when we find ourselves in a tight situation (trouble).

Is it possible to question the Lord, to dissent with His decision? I'm not talking about complaining or arguing because your flesh wants something other than what you have. I'm speaking of legitimately bring a concern to God and asking Him to look at it again. This is much like filing a motion in court before a judge. To do so, you must have grounds or new evidence and information to support your claim. King Hezekiah had been given a death sentence. The prophet Isaiah was instructed by God to go to the king and tell him to prepare his house (affairs) because he was going to die (Isa. 38). Most people would either do just that, accepting death, or yell, scream and cry at God, claiming that He is unfair or even turning their backs on Him because they didn't like His judgment. Instead, Hezekiah turned his face to the wall. In other words, he looked away from every distraction and circumstance he was facing in order to talk to the Lord and plead his case. God is not against us presenting our case to Him for further consideration. In fact, He delights in it. Isaiah 1:18 tells us that it is actually God's idea. He longs to meet with us face to face and to have us reason with Him. Having fear of the Lord doesn't mean we are afraid or intimidated, unable to approach God; rather it means that we revere Him and have an awesome dread of displeasing Him. Hezekiah asked God to remember the way he had served Him and of their relationship. He asked the Lord to remember his loyal heart. This is, I believe, the key to being able to present our case before God. It's not that we have never made mistakes or failed as we follow God, but that our hearts are peaceable and quiet before Him, seeking His way and trusting His leading. Psalm 24:3–5 states that the one who can ascend to the hill of the Lord (His dwelling place) is the one with clean hands (repentance) and a pure heart. In fact, God desires to show Himself strong on behalf of those who come to Him (2 Chronicles 16:9). The old commercial which that "membership has its rewards" was definitely on to something! Abiding with God enables us to talk and listen, to reason with Him and see change come about. King Hezekiah not only received his petition (to lengthen his life), but also received the guarantee that God would protect and deliver his city from the hands of their enemy (Isa.

38:5–6). It was a testimony not only to those of the house of Israel, but to unbelievers all around.

Father, I repent of the times I felt I had to do things on my own, without consulting You or Your Word. There is no way that I could ever bring about either rest or restoration in my situation in my own strength. I ask that You teach me to submit myself to You, making Your will and plan for me my focus and priority. As I do, I trust You to bring about complete restoration in my life, in Jesus' name.

Chapter 9

Remain

It is not enough to simply learn to enter into rest, we need to be able to remain in that place, wholly submitted and focused on Him, despite what goes on around us. The fight for us, then, is to enter and remain. This is the good fight of faith. 1 Timothy 6:12 urges us to compete, contend, labor and fervently strive (fight) for the beautiful, valuable and worthy (good) contest, effort or race (fight). Our sole job is to remain in Him, maintaining a complete reliance on and confession of His truth and not allowing anyone or anything to move us from that place.

Dwelling in the presence of God provides a respite for us. It allows us to stop doing things that we are not designed to do (worrying, being afraid, fighting our own battles) and that are therefore difficult and unpleasant. In Him, we come to a place of trust, a shelter where we can rest. Once here, He can show us where we need to make adjustments so we can go even deeper into Him. Webster's Dictionary defines the word *dwell* as "to remain, to live as a resident, to keep the attention directed at something." The definition implies that dwelling includes the need to continue. This is a key to experiencing God's rest in life in a lasting way. In the midst of the trials and troubles that we encounter daily in this world, it's important that we have a relationship with the One who never fails or falters. We can confidently rest in the Lord, despite what goes on around us. In fact, He promises to hold us in the palm of His hand so that the enemy can't snatch us from Him (John 10:28). When we place our life in His hands and trust in Him, the very mountains will depart and the hills will be removed but His kindness (favor, mercy) will never depart from us. In fact, we have a covenant (binding agreement) of peace that will never be removed (Isa. 54:10). When we take our place in Christ and rest in the fullness of what He has done for us, He establishes us in righteousness and places us far from oppression. Abiding in Him gives us the ability to remain under cover, protected from every device and strategy the enemy tries to bring against us (Ps. 91:4–10).

Remaining in Him requires that we consciously and continually purpose to keep our focus on Him, not just once a day or once a week, but repeatedly. Everyone knows that just because you brush your teeth in the morning it doesn't mean they don't need to be brushed again in the evening, and so forth every day. We would never believe that our teeth (or hair, or bodies) would remain clean if we only brushed or washed once. Why then do we suppose that to seek God or enter His presence once or infrequently is enough? In the book of 2 Chronicles we see this principle displayed in the life of Asa, King of Judah. He started out well. He was very zealous for the Lord and did what was right and pleasing to God (2 Chron. 14:2–3), and commanded the people of Judah to seek God and follow His law (2 Chron. 14:4). What was the result of seeking God and removing every idol and false object of worship? The kingdom was quiet, fortified (protected) and had rest and no war. In fact, Asa directly attributed Judah's peace and prosperity to seeking the Lord (2 Chron. 14:7). They built and prospered because of their intimate relationship with God. They were abiding in Him. When enemies tried to come against them, Asa and the people of Judah remained safely in the secret place, hidden and resting in His power (2 Chron. 14:11). In fact, as Asa cried out to God, he proclaimed that the nation was resting on Him. What a wonderful depiction of the benefits of knowing and relying on God. But, this behavior must be habitual. It is not enough to do it once or even for a season. Our relationship with God must be intimate and it must be ongoing. Just as we brush our teeth and feed our bodies daily, we must put a priority on seeking the Lord through prayer and the study of His Word *daily.*

Smith Wigglesworth famously said that most Christians feed their bodies three hot meals a day but only feed their spirits one cold snack a week. This ought not be the case for believers. We are to require Him like we require air! He alone is our strength and our song (Ps. 118:14), our shield, fortress and Deliverer (Ps. 144:2). In him is everything we need pertaining to life and godliness (2 Pet. 1:3). Given this, why do we still suppose that we can get by in our own strength and ability? The answer is when we prosper, when things are going well and when we are free from worry and attack we forget that our strength comes from Him. We get comfortable and begin to believe our own press, thinking that somehow we have accomplished these things ourselves. The prophet Azariah warned Asa that the Lord would be with him as long as he was with the Lord. Azariah was definitely not describing a casual, occasional relationship. The opposite of the kind of relationship Azariah described is forsaking the Lord and that choice brings its own kind of consequences. Unfortunately, Asa did not continue to fully trust and rely on God and the consequences of his choice not only brought war and famine, but eventually his own death. The worst part is that it happened gradually—the once zealous king took the words of the prophet and acted on them faithfully but only for a time. But as other priorities crept in and peace and prosperity lulled him to sleep, he forgot. You might say he never saw what was coming. It is said that history repeats itself because we do not learn from it. Let us not make the same mistake.

It's important to learn how to remain in a place of supernatural rest during times of upheaval. Daniel and the three Hebrew children (Shadrach, Meshach and Abed-Nego) were alive during a time of great turmoil. A foreign army had overrun their nation and they, along with all their valuables, were taken from their homes and land and brought to serve King Nebuchadnezzar. They had little to no knowledge of the culture or manners of this society and in fact they were enemies of the state. On top of this, they were instructed by those in charge that they had to eat and drink things that were against their beliefs. Daniel and his friends, however, had purposed (committed) in their hearts that they would not defile themselves by eating the king's food. You might think, "It's only food, and they were prisoners; what's the big deal?" Their unwillingness to compromise their beliefs was the very act of obedience that opened the door for God to move them into a position of favor and influence and authority. He did this in a foreign land where they were prisoners and didn't know the language or customs! How was this possible? They were at rest in Him; resting in their faith, resting in their intimate knowledge of their God and what He was able to do for and through them for His glory. Because they knew Him, they were able to rest and put their trust in His ability to handle every situation and circumstance they encountered. He gave them all the answers they needed at exactly the right times so they could show those who had initially been their enemies the omnipotence of the Lord, the only true God. When it appeared that only compromise would bring them safety and longevity, their commitment to their faith and their willingness to obey in the face of adversity, resting and trusting in His faithfulness, is what brought about victory, time after time. The same is true for His disciples today.

Remaining in God's rest requires us to keep our focus on Him regardless of what is going on. Sometimes we need reminders. My kitchen counter is often littered with sticky notes to remind me of important things I don't want to forget. We have alarms on our phones and pop-up reminders on our computers. The busier things are, the more we have on our minds and the more likely we are to forget. I don't know about you, but for me it is downright aggravating to forget things, especially small, simple things. Our enemy, the devil, uses our "forgetfulness" to his full advantage. He delights in getting us so caught up in the details, in putting out proverbial fires, that we miss the big picture. So what is the big picture? We have a loving and wonderful Father God who has paid the price through the shed blood of His Son Jesus Christ and He will provide for all of our needs—financial, physical, and psychological. The list is infinite. God has already given us the victory in every area because Jesus is the Name above *all* names! So, we need to remember what it says in Psalm 116:7–8, "return to your rest o my soul, for the Lord has dealt bountifully with you." In other words, we need to remember that our position in victory requires us to rest in Him, trusting in His faithfulness and ability and studying and declaring His Word. He is the One who has delivered our soul from death (ruin), our eyes from weeping and our feet from falling (Ps. 116:8). When all seems chaotic and confusion sets in, this is our reminder—our alarm, our sticky note—telling us that the enemy is trying to get us out of our position of rest. The devil wins when we come out of the arena of faith and into the arena of flesh, when we leave from resting in Him and look for alternative solutions. But, when we learn to remain steadfast in our fellowship and trust in the faithfulness of our Heavenly Father He is able to give us resounding victory on every front.

We are not in this alone. God is with us every step of the way and He always has a plan to bring us through victoriously. We know from Jeremiah 29:11 that He always has a plan to bring us to a successful and longed for end. Still, we often question what the plan is when we are in the midst of a storm or trial. At times, getting to the end seems unfathomable due to the howl of the wind and the sheer size of the waves. God has a plan to take care of us and carry us through the storm. Jeremiah 31:25 declares that He satiates the weary soul and replenishes every sorrowful soul. He sees us in our need and has already made provision for us. The words used in this verse speak to abundance and not just merely getting by—God will fill us up to overflowing, abundantly waters us, and satisfies every need. We can rest in Him knowing that He desires better than good for us, He wants us fully satisfied.

Another benefit for those who remain in His presence is found in Paul's second letter to the Corinthian church. Second Corinthians 3:17 tells us that where the Spirit of the Lord is, there is liberty. In other words, we are free, unrestrained, unbound—slaves to nothing! How can we enjoy this freedom, this position of liberty? We have to be where the Spirit of the Lord is. The Bible says that when we get saved, He dwells in us (John 14:17). So why, then, are most Christians not experiencing the liberty from pain, stress, depression, or physical ailments that we have been promised? The answer is because we have missed dwelling in Him. John 14 speaks of the gift of His peace (John 14:27), which is a peace unlike anything the world could ever give us. How can we access this peace? By fellowshipping with the Holy Spirit, who longs to teach us all things (John 14:26). This peace that He offers keeps our hearts from being troubled or afraid. When we abide with Him, this peace, along with joy, love and provision, is ours for the asking (John 14:7). God isn't keeping peace *from* us, He's keeping it *for* us, drawing us into the secret place, safe from the storms of life and the enemy's reach. God longs for us to enter into His presence and rest in His peace.

The path to His rest is important for us to find. It matters how and where we walk. I'm not just speaking of the physical act of walking, although that goes without saying. It also truly matters whether or not we align ourselves with the world or with Him. Will we choose to "go with the flow" of the world, forever losing ground as we drift along with the current of popular opinion and political correctness, or will we make the effort to stand for right and Truth? Jeremiah the prophet admonishes believers to "Stand at the crossroads and look; ask for the ancient paths, ask where the good way is, and walk in it." Why? Because it is there that we will find rest for our souls (Jer. 6:16). Our rest, our peace depends on finding out what Truth is (the Word, God's eternal ways) and walking in it! Rest requires effort on our part! We do need to strive and struggle in our own strength, but we must do the work of committing to diligently studying His Word and to using it as a compass for our life. Why? Because if we don't, we will miss it. It's that simple! Matthew 7:13–14 issues this warning: "Enter by the narrow gate, for wide is the gate and broad is the way that leads to destruction and there are many who go in by it. Because narrow is the gate and difficult is the way which leads to life and there are few who find it." Be diligent to search out the path that God has and wisely choose to follow it. You will never regret your decision—it has eternal implications.

What are we to do once we find the "old path?" How are we to ensure that we remain on it? Have you ever heard the expression "Set your face like flint?" It may seem a bit antiquated, but in these times, it is something that we as children if God must learn to do. This phrase speaks of determination and an unwillingness to let go, despite what our feelings tell us or the circumstances pressing against us look like. Isaiah 50:7 references this term. We are only able to set our faces like flint when we know beyond a shadow of a doubt that the Lord God is with us, that He will help us. When we abide in Him, we know that we are hidden in the secret place of the Most High, that we are covered underneath His wings and that He is our refuge and fortress. We are able to rest knowing that He is our shield and buckler and that we will not be moved and no evil shall befall us (Ps. 91). Isaiah 50:7 tells us that because God helps us, we will not be disgraced. It is because we put our trust completely in Him that we shall not be ashamed. When we learn Who He truly is, all that He has done, and who He has made us to be in Christ, we can hold fast to this. We can line our words and our will up to His and confidently say, "the Lord is on my side, I will not fear (dread, tremble, be afraid), what can man do to me" (Ps. 118:6). Instead of running, we can stand firm in the knowledge that the Lord is our strength and our song (praise) and He has become our salvation in every situation (Ps. 118:14).

Is it possible to be at peace even when things look bad and there is much resistance against us? Second Thessalonians 3:13 instructs us not to grow weary in doing good (the right thing). But how can we do this? It's natural to get tired and become discouraged when facing stressful circumstances and opposition. And the key word is natural. When we make the Lord our dwelling place, however, entering into the secret place by maintaining close fellowship with Him through the Word and prayer, things change from *natural* to *supernatural* in our lives. We are no longer the ones trying to face our situations head on. Instead, as we rest in Him, He (the God of peace Himself) gives us peace *always* in *every way* (v.16). So when we feel stressed out, discouraged and like we want to quit, we can exchange our ability for His ability and rest in the knowledge that He is taking care of things. We can have assurance of the Lord's help when we know Him and abide in His presence. One place His promise of help is documented is in Isaiah 42:16. The Lord declares that He will bring the blind by a way (path) they did not know, and lead them in paths unknown. What causes the blind to become blind? The enemy loves nothing better than to bring confusion, upset, stress and deception into our lives. Because we live in a fallen world, this is "legal" but we don't have to accept what the devil brings. Even in the darkest of situations, the promise in verse 16 enables us to rest in Him, for He will lead us, even when we are unable to see the road. In fact, He promises to make darkness light before us, and crooked places straight. He declares that He will do these things for His disciples and not forsake them. So, no matter what we are facing, what darkness seems to prevail, when we abide in Him, we can rest, knowing that He is not a man who lies or a son of man who changed His mind (Num. 23:19).

Philippians 4:4 instructs us to rejoice in the Lord always. In other words, we are to be cheerful, calmly happy, and joyful at all times. But what about when bad things happen, when people don't treat us right, or when we encounter challenging situations? If we read further, Paul shows us the key to rejoicing always. Philippians 4:6–7 tell us that we are to be anxious for nothing, instead bringing every need and concern to God in prayer and being thankful to Him for the answers. As we fellowship and spend time with Him, His very own peace, which our minds and natural understanding can't begin to comprehend, will guard around our hearts and minds through Christ Jesus. God is telling us that spending time with Him will be like having our very own safe room—no person or thing can penetrate the peace that surrounds us and the joy we experience by remaining in His place of rest.

The ability to enter into rest and to remain there is dependent on our knowledge of Who He is and our trust in Him. Can we trust Him and what He's promised even when the time line doesn't match up to what we think it should? Do we truly believe that He is faithful and good, no matter how He works things out? Or are we merely interested in "trusting" when things seem to go according to our plan? Jairus had a big need—his daughter was dying (Matt. 8:18–26). He did all the right "faith things"—he sought Jesus, he confessed his belief that Jesus could make his daughter well, and he began to lead Him to where his daughter was. Then, they were interrupted. The woman with the issue of blood seemingly got in the way of his miracle. Did Jairus become angry, did he yell at her to wait her turn, did he give up on his miracle and stop believing due to the delay? No, he remained in faith, believing that Jesus knew what He was doing and that His miracle-working power was still effectively working on his daughter's behalf. Our finite minds must be renewed in His Word and His presence to comprehend His infinite power. Only then can we truly rest in Him, knowing beyond any shadow of a doubt that He is faithful.

The ability to remain in His presence affects our ability to contend with the devil. In Ephesians 6, we see Paul's directive to the New Testament church regarding spiritual warfare. Ephesians 6:10 admonishes us to "be strong in the Lord and in the power of His might." What does this mean? How can we accomplish this? In order to gain more clarity, it will be helpful to look at each word in an expanded form, as found in the Strong's Concordance. The word strong means to empower, enable, or increase in strength. It is derived from a word that means a fixed position (in place, time or state), i.e. one of rest. It seems that as we remain fixed in Him, at rest in His presence, we increase in strength and are empowered to fight. What exactly is the "power of His might?" Power means vigor, dominion, might and strength. Might means forcefulness, ability, mighty power and strength. When we rest in Him, we experience the dominion of His mighty power and strength in a forceful way! Paul goes on to tell the church to put on the whole armor of God so that they may be able to stand against the wiles (strategies) of the devil. It sounds like God already knows the strategies of the devil and has weapons to counteract them, to bring about our victory. One of these weapons is the "shoes of peace" (Eph. 6:15). We are to have our feet shod with the gospel of peace. We are instructed to stand on this. After all, we stand on our feet and no other body part. God takes this peace thing seriously and so should we! It is an integral part of the armor and strategy that He has provided for us to enable us to hold up under the enemy's attacks and come out victorious.

Stephen was a man who knew how to rest. He was chosen by the apostles to serve not only because of his good reputation (character) but also because he was full of the Holy Spirit. Stephen must have spent time abiding with Him, as others plainly saw the effect. Acts 6:8 tells us that Stephen was full of faith and power, doing wonders and signs among the people. Here was an ordinary man doing extraordinary works. How? He regularly spent time in fellowship with God and because he did, God gave him power to perform supernatural acts as a testimony. Even as he was being stoned to death (Acts 7:54–60), he did not leave His place of rest. Rather, Stephen was so close to God, abiding under the shadow of the Almighty, that he had an open vision and pleaded with God to have mercy on the very ones who were killing him. Now that is a picture of how to remain in rest and experience God's plan and purpose in your life.

In the fourth chapter of the book of Ephesians, Paul urges the church to walk and be worthy (appropriately) of the calling that God placed on them (Eph. 4–1). What is this calling? It is Spiritual unity. God has called the New Testament church to be unified in one Spirit and purpose—to establish His Kingdom (His way of doing and being) on the earth. In Ephesians 4:2–3, he tells us how to do this—with humility and patience, keeping unity through the bond (control) of peace. Peace is a central factor to maintaining the unity that is so vital to fulfilling God's call for the church both individually and corporately on the earth. This is not just a lack of quarreling; it is the deep, abiding peace of God. The Greek word is eirene, which means prosperity, peace, quietness, rest, and wholeness. In order to function properly and effectively, we must learn to rest. When we enter into this type of rest through intimate fellowship with the Holy Spirit and the Word of God, we no longer feel the need to compete with other members or other parts of the body of Christ. We aren't concerned with anything other than fulfilling the call and purpose that God has placed on our life and we don't compare ourselves to others. This is why peace is so essential to maintaining unity in the Body of Christ. Without it, the devil can easily run us aground on the rocks of competition, jealousy and infighting, thwarting the essential purpose of the church in this world.

For centuries there has been much speculation about the return of Christ, leading to disputes and even church splits. Without a doubt, time is winding down. As described in Matthew 24, wars, pestilence and famine are prevalent in the world today. Unfortunately, so are offense, lawlessness and the loss of the love of God in how people treat others. Matthew 24:13 says that those who endure to the end shall be saved. Does this mean that those who by force of their will and sheer determination survive the horrors of the end times will make it to heaven? No, not exactly. According to the Strong's Concordance, the word *endure* means to stay under, hold out under stress, persevere under pressure, remain, abide, and wait calmly and courageously. This reflects more than just patience or passive resignation—it shows active, energetic resistance to defeat and the ability to calmly and bravely endure. Where does this ability come from? It comes from remaining, abiding and staying under. In other words, it comes from knowing how to get into the secret place and stay there. In order to remain strong and true to the Lord until the end, Christians must know how to enter into rest and remain in His presence. Only then can we successfully complete our assignment. Matthew 24:46 says that those whom the Master finds doing things according to His plan will be blessed (well off, fortunate, and happy). The secret to happiness and well-being? Resting in the secret place, where God provides all we need to endure to the end.

The book of the Revelation clearly tells us that there is coming a time when the world will experience terrible tragedies, both natural and relational. There will be wars, famines, plagues, earthquakes and many other devastating events experienced at the end of the age. One sign of the end times will be the loss of peace. In fact, Revelation 6 speaks of this in verse 4. In the vision presented here, John sees what is commonly referred to as the four horsemen of the Apocalypse (great, cataclysmic disaster). The second horseman is granted the ability to take peace from the earth, causing the inhabitants to kill one another. This power is real, whether we believe the horseman to be literal or figurative. Headlines from many recent national tragedies highlight unrest, upheaval and a seemingly inexplicable desire to shed blood. The word kill in this verse is a Greek word meaning to butcher, slaughter, maim, wound and slay. When peace is removed, this is what ensues. How are we to combat this darkness that is invading our culture and world? The Bible makes it clear that as Christians, we are ambassadors of Heaven in this world but we are not of (belonging to, resembling) this world (1 John 4; James 4). We are to hold fast to the profession (confession) of our faith. This means that we are to seize upon and not turn loose our knowledge and identification with the One who Himself became our peace. Our confession of faith is our access to salvation through Jesus Christ. The word salvation (sozo) encompasses prosperity, healing, deliverance, wholeness, and peace—everything that is ours because of the death, burial, and resurrection of Jesus Christ. When we allow Jesus lordship in our lives, confessing Him as Lord and Master, we enter into our position of rest in all He has accomplished. From this position, we are able to hold fast to every benefit. He is our peace in the midst of every storm—whether natural or relational. As we maintain our grip on this (faith), God maintains His grip on us (grace), and we are able to walk in and exhibit His peace, no matter what the world is dishing out.

Paul's letters to the church at Thessalonica (1 and 2 Thessalonians) can seem overwhelming, especially to those of us living in what most definitely appears to be the end times, with wars, famine, and lawlessness. The darkness of the world keeps getting darker, but we are instructed to keep shining our light and to not grow weary in doing good (2 Thess. 3:13). How can we maintain our joy, strength and hope in the midst of this perverse generation? By knowing the Lord of peace. In 2 Thessalonians 3:16, Paul prays that the Lord of peace Himself would give us peace always, in every way. Sounds good, doesn't it? But do we truly understand what he is saying? The Lord of peace gives us peace. When and how? Always, in every way. So, the supreme authority of peace gives us His version of peace, always and thoroughly, in His style and character. Whew! Now that's peace! It obviously doesn't concern Paul that all hell will literally be breaking loose in the last days, because what God Himself is able to bring to the church, to every believer who will seek Him, is His own peace, which is so complete and so powerful that we will know that He is with us, through every situation and trial. His quietness and rest are to be the supreme authority governing us during this time. The catch? We must seek Him and learn to enter into His rest through fellowship with the Holy Spirit in the name of Jesus. There is no other way to an abiding, all-encompassing peace.

During the days of Isaiah the prophet, the world was much like it is today, but not in the sense of our modern conveniences or technological breakthroughs. It was like our world in terms of the underlying current of darkness and depravity. In fact, Isaiah pronounced woe (judgment) on those who call evil good, darkness light, bitter sweet, and who are wise in their own eyes, departing from the Word and ways of God (Isa. 5:20–21). Sound familiar? We live in a culture of situational ethics, where there are no "absolutes" and instead there is only what seems or feels right at the time. We have stopped seeking His Truth and come up with our own, apart from His wisdom and counsel. The Word goes on to say that we are to hallow and fear (revere, respect, be in awe of) the Lord only. To those who do, to His true disciples, He will be a sanctuary, but to those who do not seek Him and revere Him, He will be a stone of stumbling. Many shall stumble, fail, be broken, snared, and taken (Isa. 8:13–15). How do we make sure that we are not among those deceived and trapped in false beliefs and darkness? We do this by waiting on Him and having hope in Him (Isa. 8:17). There is truly no peace or wisdom apart from the Lord. Waiting on Him, abiding in His presence and studying His Word has benefits; not only do we come to know Him intimately, but we gain strength and endurance for the journey we are taking (Isaiah 40:28–31). The result? When we seek Him and stand for Him, we become signs and wonders; we become a testimony to a fallen and deeply troubled world that our God is faithful and that He reigns in all power and glory. Our abiding in Him allows the fullness of His power to be displayed through us as we rest in His Lordship.

Have you ever wondered why it seems impossible for the world to achieve any lasting peace? Why can't the intellectuals and leaders of the world institute policies or treaties that will bring about lasting peace? The answer is because our humanness is in the way. There is no way that we, as humans can effect lasting peace because of the war going on inside us as a result of sin. Apart from a life lived in Christ, we are unable to achieve true, lasting peace. Isaiah 32:17–18 gives us a key to experiencing peace that endures. This scripture tells us that the work (product, possession, business) of righteousness will be peace, and the effect of righteousness will be quietness and assurance forever. In other words, if we seek to remain in perpetual peace, righteousness must be in place. We know, that when Adam sinned, we fell from the position of righteousness (right standing) that we had with God because sin entered the world through his disobedience. All who followed were born into this sin. Because of Adam's sin, sin rules in our world, but because of the death, burial and resurrection of Jesus Christ, the power of sin was broken and we can reign (have authority) in life by receiving Him and His righteousness (Rom. 5:17). In other words, when we choose to forsake our way, our thoughts, and our fleshly desires and submit to Him, all His attributes, including righteousness, become ours. As we remain in Him, seeking first His kingdom (rule and reign) and His righteousness, everything we need is added to us (Matt. 6:33). Isaiah 32:18 tells us that God's people, the ones who exchange their sinful natures and take on the righteousness provided by His Son, will dwell in peaceful habitations and secure dwellings (place of residence), enjoying quiet resting places.

What other benefits can we expect from remaining in God's rest? Is it possible to avoid falling into the schemes and snares that the enemy sets for us? Absolutely! How is this accomplished? The Bible tells us in Galatians 5:16 that if we walk in the Spirit we will not fulfill the lust of the flesh. In other words, as we take our place in Christ by getting to know who we are and what belongs to us and by continually following after and being obedient to the Holy Spirit, we will not complete, perform or accomplish the things our fleshly nature wants to do. Instead, when we refuse to listen to the demands of our bodies and minds we will be able to remain in a position of rest, no matter what the devil throws in our path. Galatians 5:24–25 go on to say that if we are Christ's (born again), our flesh (passions and desires) will be crucified (extinguished and subdued)! We are to keep step with and conform to the Spirit of God in an orderly fashion. We can't accomplish this kicking and screaming. Only when we choose to abide in Him will we be able to truly walk as He walks.

God is looking for a people who will abide with Him; those who will seek to know Him in the beauty of His holiness, to be intimately acquainted with His Word and His ways. The second chapter of Malachi shows us what God desires in a relationship with His children. He desires to have a covenant (binding relationship) giving life and peace to us and in return we are to fear (reverence) Him. We are to have the law of truth in our mouths and iniquity (evil, wickedness) is to be far from us. This will allow us to walk in peace and equity before Him. The ability to enjoy this type of relationship is contingent upon abiding in Him. It is not enough to merely enter into His presence occasionally when we are weary and need refilling. We must continually and on a daily basis seek Him and become intimately acquainted with His Spirit by studying His Word. His command to abide in Him (John 15:4) was just that—a command. God knows that outside of a life hidden in Him, we are unable to produce the righteous fruits of Kingdom life! When we don't remain close to Him, we drift farther away on the current of the world. Malachi 2:8 states that because the children of Israel departed from the way, many were made to stumble. People, even the unsaved, are watching us. When we step out of His presence, when we withdraw from the pathway He has given us, when we decide to "do our own thing," we can cause others to waver and become confused and weak in their faith. We bring corruption to the body of Christ. Because we are part of the body, if infection or disease sets in, the whole body is affected. It is vital, therefore, that we remain in place and abide in His presence. In Malachi 3:7 God calls His disciples to return to Him and He promises to return to them. That is why Jeremiah declares we are to seek the Lord, to ask for the old ways and walk in them, because it is there we will find rest for our souls (Jer. 6:16).

Remember playing hide and seek when you were small? Did you have the perfect hiding spot, the one where no one could find you? God has a place like that for us, a place where we are so completely hidden in Him that the enemy can't find us. It's called the secret place, a hiding place where we are so completely wrapped up in Him that we are disguised and protected from all harm. How do we get there? By dwelling and abiding in Him, by sitting down and remaining in His presence, refusing to be dislodged from His covering. Is it tempting to "peek out" and see what's going on when we are hidden? Yes, but rest assured that staying permanently wrapped up in Christ is God's plan for you and He will reveal everything you need to know at the proper time. His rest is the position of abiding with Him (2 Chronicles 20; Psalm 91; Hebrews 3 and 4; John 15). It is impossible to enter into His rest if we don't spend time with Him. When we spend time with Him, unbelief disappears and we are ushered into the place of rest, from which we can watch God work supernatural victories on our behalf. Now that is a place to remain and make your dwelling place.

Lord, I ask that you teach me to remain in your place of rest, to keep my focus on You rather than being swayed by what goes on around me. Help me to dwell in Your secret place, the place that the enemy can't find me!

Chapter 10

Abide

During a time of prayer, God spoke to me and said that I, by myself, determine how much His presence is poured out in my life and that together, we determine how much his presence is poured out on this earth. This was a stunning revelation, after all, God can do as He pleases, right?! He showed me a large gate, which had a rope and pulley system attached. He explained that this was the floodgate of Heaven and that in order to open it, a threshold must be met. The threshold is reached through worship, acknowledging Who He is, and creating a connection to Him. God went on to explain that when the threshold is met it opens the floodgate, which allows the miraculous to occur because every resource of Heaven is then available for the receiving. I saw myself praising and worshipping Him, declaring Who He is, all His wonderful attributes and accomplishments, His marvelous character, and glorifying His name, His Word, and

His ability. As I did this, the floodgate was raised, allowing His presence to spill forth onto the earth and onto my circumstances and life. However, as I slowed down or stopped, the floodgate closed and the threshold had to be met again to re-open the gate. I sensed that it would be much easier to sustain my praise and thanksgiving than to work from "scratch" each time. As we sustain our connection to Him by acknowledging continually Who He is, we come into proper alignment and gain accurate perspective. In this position, we are able to remain in an attitude of worship and entertain His presence continually. It is then that the floodgates of Heaven remain open and His provision is available to us to meet every need (Jer. 9:24). This, He told me, is what it means to abide.

What does God want to get through to us about abiding in Him? God's intention for his children is peace. Jeremiah 29:11 declares that He knows the thoughts He has toward us. These are not just any plans, but rather plans for peace, not plans for evil. Knowing this should pretty much lay to rest the belief that God puts suffering and hardship on His children to teach them something. That said, however, we can always learn something when the enemy brings something against us and we can turn the situation around to glorify God. This verse also tells us that God plans for our future and will bring us to an expected end. How, then, do we access this God-ordained future? Jeremiah 29:12–13 reveal the answer to us: we are to call to God, go to Him and pray to Him. We are also instructed to seek Him with all our heart. The key to finding God is to fully apply ourselves to spending time in fellowship with Him and to make this our quest and our life's aim. When we place ourselves in this position, God listens to our petitions and brings us back from the captivity the enemy has tried to impose on us (Jer. 29:14). The key to answered prayer and rest have been there all along—it is abiding in His presence.

Abiding in Him is something we must focus on. The events and issues swirling all around us in the world and repeated ad nauseam by every news source and social media outlet can be overwhelming, causing problems to seem enlarged and overshadowing what we know to be true. This is absolutely the tactic of the devil—to make the evil seem like it can, and will, triumph over truth and good. We, as believers, know from the Word that this is not so, but our enemy attempts to throw us off-balance by bombarding us from every angle with situations that make us feel helpless and hopeless. What are we to do to combat the enemy's onslaught to our faith? We are to seek the Lord, to follow after righteousness and to look upon the Rock from which we were hewn (Isa. 51:1–3). In other words, instead of letting ourselves be swept away by the evil, the hatred, the seemingly insurmountable problems that face us, our nation, and our world, we are to keep our focus on the Lord, our Father, the One who is all-powerful. Isaiah goes on to instruct us to look to Abraham, who is our father in faith (Rom. 4:16). God uses Abraham and his wife

Sarah as examples to us, for through all their struggles and trials He blessed and increased them. If He did it for them, as they walked in faith, focusing on the promise instead of the problem, He will surely do it for us, for God is not a respecter of persons (Rom. 2:11). If He did it for others, He will do it for us, because of our faith.

What does God promise to those of us who abide in Him, seek Him and look to Him as their Rock and refuge? He declares that He will comfort us in the waste places and make our deserts and wildernesses like Eden. Joy, gladness, singing and thanksgiving will be ours (Isa. 51:3), even in the time of trouble, if we abide in and place our trust in Him. When our hearts are overwhelmed, we can cry out to God and He will lead us to Him. He is our Rock (refuge) and He is higher than us or any circumstance we encounter (Ps. 61:2).

This world is so fast-paced and hectic. It's easy to put things off, especially things without specific deadlines screaming for our immediate attention—things like studying the Word of God and prayer, for example. After all, God understands, right? He knows how busy our schedules are and knows we only have so many hours in a day. We have become slaves of our schedules, unable to break free to spend time on what really matters. Or perhaps unwilling is a better word than unable. After all, we make time for what is truly important to us. We make sure that we get some "me time" because after all, we deserve it, especially since we are so busy and work so hard. But, God is unimpressed with this. In fact, in Jeremiah 6:10–14 He calls people like this "uncircumcised in ear." In other words, people like this don't listen to Him and don't heed His warnings. This passage of scripture isn't talking about unbelievers, but rather God's people who have drifted away from what is truly important—God's Word and His ways. This happens when we allow our priorities to change and become distracted by the natural to the neglect of the supernatural. When our focus turns from Him to the world around us, we begin to live out of our flesh rather than our spirit. We become covetous and begin to live falsely, according to our sinful human nature (Jer. 6:13). In this condition we are no longer able to bring true peace to others, or ourselves because that is only found by dwelling with Him, in His presence. The answer to this problem is to return to Him and place a high priority on spending time in the Word and in prayer. As we abide in Him and His Word abides in us, we can bear much fruit. When we neglect to make abiding a priority, when we operate without Him, we can do nothing (John 15:5).

What about the times when we mess up and fail to do what He asks? Or what if we fail to ask Him and act on our own wisdom? We can certainly make a mess of things quickly when left to our own devices. I'm so thankful that God is patient and loving! He desires to show His children mercy and grace. But, there is a condition that must be met to experience these—we must wait on Him. Isaiah 30:18 tells us that the Lord will indeed wait so that He may be gracious to us. He is waiting for us to come to Him in order to show His grace to us. When we come and exalt Him, He shows His mercy toward us. Why do we need to come to Him and lift Him up? After all, if He's God He can show us favor and grace if He wants to, right? That is true, but He is also a God of justice (Isa. 30:18) who is bound by this. He is under no obligation to "bless our mess." It is when we realize that we need Him desperately and turn our focus and our lives to Him, seeking Him and making Him our top priority, that we are blessed. As we wait for the Lord, we will find that He has been waiting for us all along.

If you are anything like me, you may have experienced going "around the mountain" more than once. This is when you get the chance to go through something again in order to have a potentially different outcome—a chance to retake the test and score higher, so to speak. If so, maybe you can relate to this: Have you ever worked at something and it seemed that the harder you worked, the more difficult things became to accomplish? This is typically accompanied by a proportional increase in frustration levels. The kingdom of God doesn't operate the way we would think it should; in fact, Isaiah 55:9 tells us that God's ways and thoughts are higher than ours, even as the heavens are far above the earth. This should give us a clue that, as citizens of Heaven, we can't do things the same way the world does and achieve success. In the thirtieth chapter of Isaiah, God gives us a key to victory as well as a warning. God is telling Israel (and us!)

in this chapter that the key to our success and our salvation is found in returning and resting (Isa. 55:15). This is a powerful Kingdom truth! He goes on to say that our strength is found in quietness and confidence. In other words, as we are faithful to enter into His presence, the secret place, and settle down, resting and trusting in His victory and authority over every situation, we encounter our help, rescue, defense and victory. Just like in 2 Chronicles 20, the Lord will fight for us and do a better job vanquishing our adversaries than we could ever do in our own strength. And the bonus is that we will emerge not only victorious, but peaceful and rested, not even "smelling of smoke," so to speak (Dan. 3:27)! So God has given us the key; what is the warning? The very last sentence of Isaiah 30:15 is "but you would not." This, to me, is one of the saddest sentences in the Bible. Here God is giving us the method for successful mastery of any situation but in our humanness, we frequently reject His manner of doing things. We must learn to override our drive to demonstrate our own strength and learn to confidently trust in His. When we enter into rest, we allow God to show Himself strong on our behalf, and the victory is sure.

Unfortunately, waiting is something I've never been particularly good at. I get so excited about things that are to happen that I see myself already in the situation, doing whatever it is. Imagine my shock at the realization that I am, in fact, not there yet, but instead I am still here, waiting. It is especially tempting for us, as Christians, to focus on Jesus' glorious return, when He comes riding on the clouds, trumpets blaring to signal the end of this age and take His people to heaven and imagine ourselves already there. We need to remind ourselves (often) that there are things for us to do in the here and now, despite any darkness or difficulty we may encounter. Psalm 62 demonstrates *how* we are to wait. In fact, the word wait doesn't mean to merely pass time. Instead, it means to be astonished, to cease, to hold peace, to quiet, to rest, and to stand still. This is a lot different than our modern-day definition of waiting. Psalm 62:5 says that we are to wait silently for God alone, for our expectation is from Him alone. In other words, we are to rest in Him, focused and expectant because He alone has what we need and desire. Isaiah 65:6 goes on to say that God alone is our rock, our salvation and our defense (inaccessible place), therefore we shall not be moved. Waiting on Him obviously has its benefits! In Him we find our salvation and our glory. (Isa. 65:7). Verse 8 summarizes our instructions—we are to trust in God at all times, even when we don't "feel" like it, and pour out our hearts before Him. When we do, we find that we are positioned in a place of strength and protection, hidden in Him. It is here that we find our greatest victory.

David knew the secret of strength; he knew where to run for protection and provision. He also knew how to enter that place. Psalm 26 finds David talking to his God. He is asking God to examine and prove his heart and mind (Ps. 26:2). Why would David ask this? He asked this because he knew that

God would let him know if any corrections or adjustments were needed in order to line up with God's expectations of him. You see, David was very popular, wealthy, and dynamic. It would have been easy for him to "believe his own press" and to take these qualities and use them to measure himself rather than aligning himself against God's standard. In fact, he would have been very pleased initially with the results. But God measures differently that we do. He tests the heart, examines the motives, and tries the hidden things. David could have rested in his success, his fame, his fortune, and the opinions of men, but he knew that these things would not reveal to him where he truly was in God's eyes. Instead, David sought God out, asking Him to examine his heart, motives, and actions. In fact, this was David's habit. And this is why the Bible calls David a man after God's own heart. He truly wanted to please God, not because of the benefits and the things God could do for him, but rather because of whom he knew God to be. David knew that by drawing closer and closer to the Lord, he would find his place of rest. David knew that strength and provision are found in His presence. Verse 8 of Psalm 26 declares "Lord, I have loved the habitation of Your house and the place where Your glory dwells." The most important thing to David wasn't his exploits as a warrior, his reputation as a king or the love of others. What mattered to him was being qualified to enter into the secret place and abide in the presence of his God, soaking in His glory and grace. We should align our priorities with David's example, seeking first and foremost God's glorious presence.

Doing so, however, is counter-intuitive to us in our world. Our culture prides itself on independence and self-sufficiency. We admire and esteem the "self-made" man or woman, holding them up as a model to be emulated. What happens, then, if we fall short? We feel the brunt of our failure, along with the stress of striving and the burden we have carried in our efforts. This is never God's plan for us. Instead, He encourages us to seek Him and boldly declare that He is our helper, dispelling all fear (Heb. 13:6). In other words, He is the One who is poised and ready to run to our aid and give us rest and relief in the midst of every situation. In fact, He is the God of peace who makes us complete so we can do His will, making us pleasing (fully acceptable) in His sight (Heb. 13:20–21). We do not have to fight our own battles and when we position ourselves in Christ and rest in Him, He restores, adjusts and prepares us for what He has for us. Being God-made is so much better than being self-made, because He gives us what we will need to succeed in every situation.

Have you ever wondered why Paul opened and closed so many of his letters to the New Testament church by wishing them grace and peace? Galatians 1:3 is an example of his address to those who considered him a spiritual father, the ones whom he poured his life into as he established churches throughout Asia. Paul knew better than anyone what it would take for believers to not only to survive but to thrive in their Christian faith while living in the middle of a dark pagan world. The word grace means benefit, favor, gift, joy, or pleasure and implies a divine equipping to enable one to accomplish the will of God. Peace, as we've looked at before, involves rest, quietness, prosperity, and wholeness. In other words, Paul was determined to point the believers to the Source of all success. Galatians 1:3 acknowledges that these two attributes, grace and peace, originate from the Father and are accessed through the lordship of Jesus Christ His Son through fellowship with the Holy Spirit. As we abide in Him, taking time to become intimately acquainted with the Word (Jesus) and prayer, we can enter into His rest, and therefore receive the grace we need to fulfill His call on our lives. Paul knew that the secret to not only overcoming adversity but to flourishing in an environment which was not friendly to Christianity was to stop fighting in our own strength and ability and to depend on the Lord to supply the grace and peace we so desperately need. When we follow this model, we can achieve every task He sets before us, for His glory.

You see, an abiding spirit is something He is looking for in His children. God is looking for a remnant. This term is used often when referring to the end-times but what does it really mean? In the simplest definition, a remnant is the part that is left when other parts are gone. In the book of Isaiah, the people were caught up in idolatry, in worshipping the work of their own hands, following eastern ways, and accumulating wealth for themselves (Isaiah 2:6–8). They had stepped away from God's ways to embrace the cultures around them. They had become puffed up and proud of their accomplishments, their wealth, and their positions. They were oppressive and disrespectful as a whole. Does this sound familiar? God was searching for those who would sever their ties with the world (Isa. 2:22), and return to Him. It is not enough to be in the church (during Isaiah's time, nearly all went to church) or to say a prayer of salvation. In order to become true children of the Lord, we must come out and away from the world and its ways. We must not allow ourselves to be caught up in the thought process or cultural norms of the times. Those who separate in this way, are the "remnant." When we come apart from the world, when we purposefully call on Him and abide in His presence, there is shade from the heat, shelter from the storm, and a place of refuge no matter what may come against us.

So, what do you do when the enemy surrounds you, breathing threats and intimidation, discouragement and hopelessness? That was the very situation facing the remnant of the children of God in Isaiah 37. The King of Assyria had sent his spokesperson to threaten King Hezekiah into paying tribute and basically agreeing to be taken captive. He not only spoke this to the leaders of Israel, but also to the common citizens, in order to bring fear and terror into their ranks, hoping to have the citizens exert leverage on the King, forcing his surrender. It is absolutely part of Satan's weaponry to not only bring fear and intimidation to you personally, but also to those close to you, in the hopes of inciting panic and chaos, both of which make rational thought and prayer difficult. Hezekiah knew what the ambassador said was basically true; they were outnumbered, ill-prepared and had no hope in the natural world. But, what they did have was the supernatural God of the Universe. God took the railings of the ambassador personally. Hezekiah knew that the only hope for his nation was to rely on God's strength and ability. He prayed to the Lord to save them from Assyria. He further asked that in this victory, all the nations of the earth would know that God alone was God (Isa. 37:20). Now this is a prayer that God delights to answer. In fact, 2 Chronicles 16:9 declares that the eyes of the Lord run to and fro throughout the whole earth to show Himself strong on behalf of those whose hearts are perfect toward Him! God is looking to fight the battles of His people, but we must turn to Him! When we do, He answers us as He did Hezekiah: "for I will defend (protect) this city to save it for My own sake and for My servant David's sake" (Isa 37:35). We are covenant people who are to find our protection and provision in His presence by having a heart that is quiet and friendly, while and just, and peaceable and complete before Him. No matter what the enemy whispers or shouts to intimidate you, abiding in Him is your place of defense, and God is *always victorious!*

Is it possible, then, to rest in the midst of attack and trial and when you feel overwhelmed by circumstances around you? In Micah chapter 5, we see that Israel is under siege, cut off from supplies and constantly under attack. Despite the circumstances, they are given a promise of Hope—the Messiah. Micah 5:4 tells us that Jesus shall stand and feed His followers (the flock) in the strength of the Lord. Isn't it great to know that no matter what we are going through, if we are committed and submitted to Jesus that He is there with us in the midst of our trial, feeding us and fighting for us? The verse continues by telling us that while He feeds us in the strength of the Lord, we shall abide because of His greatness and reputation to the ends of the earth. Everyone, friend and foe, will see His power and recognize His Lordship as He ministers on our behalf. Micah 5:5 goes on to describe Him as our Peace, even when the enemy enters the land. We have a promise from Him that He will never leave us or forsake us (Heb. 13:5). In the midst of trouble and unrest, we can hold fast to that promise and see the salvation of the Lord (2 Chron. 20:17).

There is indeed a great take-away in abiding. Life can get hard and situations dark. How can we know for sure the right choice, direction, or path? We must use the right compass. It is no secret that the moral compass of this world is woefully inaccurate and skewed. We can't depend on our senses, feelings or even our intellect to show us the way, for these are fallible and subject to the world's influence. Instead, we must turn to the One who never changes, who remains the same regardless of the climate of the world system. Psalm 119:105

declares that the Word of God is a lamp to our feet and a light for our path. We must use it to illuminate the darkness before us as we walk through life. It is to become our compass, always pointing to Truth, always keeping us in His will and purpose. Without abiding in Him and His Word abiding in us, we can do nothing (John 15:5). Correctly stated, we can do nothing good, beneficial or purposeful for His kingdom. In other words, anything we do in our own might or counsel will be void of His presence and power. My friends, we were not meant to live that way. We, as Kingdom subjects, were meant for more—victory, ease, favor, and blessing. How can we ensure that we remain on the mark? Psalm 16:11 tells us that when we seek Him and dwell with Him, He will show us the path of life. We don't have to guess which way to go—He will show us. The verse goes on to say that in His presence we will find fullness of joy and at His Right hand are pleasures forevermore. When we abide in His presence, we no longer need to wonder if we are going in the right direction on the right path—He makes sure of it.

Of course, anything that is a benefit to us as God's children will have a counterfeit offered by our enemy, the devil. It will be something that seems to offer promise but instead will bring pain and devastation. But surely, no one would choose the counterfeit—would they? Have you ever wondered why someone would choose an imitation over the real thing? There are many different reasons, but the Lord put a few on my heart while I was reading Jeremiah 10. In

Jeremiah 10, the Lord speaks very clearly to the prophet, instructing him not to learn the ways of the Gentiles. God revealed to me that one reason to choose an imitation over the real things is that the imitation has become familiar, routine or comfortable. Another reason we choose the imitation is because of fear. Jeremiah 10:2 also commands Jeremiah not to be dismayed of the signs of heaven. In the past, the people of Israel had failed to draw close to God, and therefore were terrified when He came down to meet with them; instead they asked Moses to meet with God and tell them what He said. Unfortunately, in their fear and lack of connection, it was easier for them to choose what they could see and touch rather than to join their hearts to the True God. The third reason some choose imitation over the real deal is that it is convenient and easier. The Gentiles would find materials around them, fashion them into a statue or idol, decorate them ornately and then worship them. God calls this vain to believe that the idols made by our own hands are anything more than art (Jer. 10:3–5). They come from man and are devoid of life. The Truth is filled with the breath of God. Truth comes straight from the Creator and is able to breathe life into every dead thing and circumstance. Jeremiah 10:10 declares that the Lord is the true God, the living God and the Everlasting King. His glory is endless, His fame is renowned and His power is limitless. When we choose to abide in Him, we choose life. Only the real can satisfy—don't choose the imitation, for true value is only found in authenticity.

There is a difference between the "peace" that can be found in the world and God's peace. The world's version is fleeting and short-lived at best, a temporary respite from all that swirls around us. God, however, has a lasting peace that is meant for His children, a peace that we can enter and remain in, no matter what is happening around us. Isaiah 26:12 speaks of this peace, telling us that God will establish it for us, for He has done all our works for us. His peace (shalom) encompasses safety, health, welfare, wholeness, prosperity, favor and rest. Nothing this world has can compare! We can tap in to this awesome peace by being diligent in seeking Him and by abiding in Him (Isa. 26:9). When we do, not only do we experience this unshakeable peace, others around us also see His judgments and learn righteousness (Isa. 26:9). It is a win-win situation and Jesus has already paid the price of entry for us. What are we waiting for?

Psalm 24:6 speaks of those who seek God. Seeking God is a habit of one who is truly a Christian. The psalm doesn't stop at verse 6 though. It goes on to detail the dynamic between the believer and God. Verses 7–10 describe believers lifting up the gates and allowing for the entrance of the King of glory. When we seek Him and humble ourselves before Him, earnestly searching out His presence, God doesn't disappoint. In fact, He brings all that He is into our midst when we throw open the doors of our hearts and lives and invite

Him to enter! And when the King of glory comes into your heart, you know it because He brings with Him all that He is—His glory, His strength, and His might. When we yield our lives to him and allow God's presence to come in, we find the everlasting door that leads us to the proper path and the narrow way. This is the old path spoken of in Jeremiah 6:16. This verse declares that when we see where the good way is and follow it, we find rest for our souls.

There are so many wonderful truths in the Word of God to be learned, so much of Him to be encountered! Where do we begin? King David gives us a wonderful example in Psalm 25:4–5. David was a man after God's own heart, not because he was perfect but because He sought after God, desiring always to know Him more. David was willing to admit his shortcomings and sins and go to God in repentance. In Psalm 25, we see David crying out to God for instruction and understanding. He asked God to show him His ways. David, more than anything, was desperate to know his God and to understand His ways so that he could walk in them! He planned to use the instruction and revelation he received as a road map for life! In fact, in verse 5 David declares that God is his salvation and asks Him to lead him in His Truth and teach him. Exactly how does David plan to learn from God and receive instruction? He positions himself in a place to receive it and he assumes a posture of waiting. In other words, David made it his purpose to abide in God's presence and to diligently seek His wisdom, His plan, and His ways until he knew Him intimately. And when he did, God showed up mightily in his life! Abiding is the secret to being taught by the Lord.

What is it that sets Christians apart from the billions of people alive today on planet earth? How can we be distinguished from the rest? It's not in our faithful attendance at a place of worship, for many world-wide do this, even in the name of false gods. It isn't the fact that we call ourselves Christians, because we have all had encounters with those who claimed His name but did not walk as He walked (Matt. 7:21–23). What sets us apart is the presence of the Lord in our lives. God spoke to Moses as a friend in Exodus 33. This great deliverer of the children of Israel and author of the Pentateuch knew the secret of the power in which he walked—fellowship with the Lord. He had a desperate need to meet with God regularly on a face-to-face basis. In fact, he took his tent outside the camp, away from the others and set it up, calling it the Tabernacle of Meeting, a place designated for meeting with the Lord, where he could fellowship with Him, seek guidance and receive strength for the journey (Exod. 33:7–11). Moses knew that the Promised Land was inhabited by people much stronger and more numerous than his people. He was not prideful enough to think that his people could journey on without the assistance and protection of the Lord, so he sought God regarding this. Moses wanted assurance that wherever they went, God would be with them. God assured Moses that His Presence would go with them and that He would give them rest. We should purpose to take the stance that Moses did and refuse to go forward if the presence of God does not go with us (Exod. 33:15). His presence in our lives is what will separate us from those who are not His, just as it did in the days of Moses (Exod. 33:16). This is our defining trait as Christians. When God is in our lives, the world will be able to tell that we have been with Him (Acts 4:13). God's goodness will be broadcast. God does not let the expectation that He be a presence in our lives slide. Jesus said that if men refused to praise Him, even the rocks would cry out, declaring His greatness. But God prefers to use people over rocks, but not just any people. God particularly likes to show His power and majesty through the lives of those who abide in His presence. Psalm 92:10 declares that God Himself exalts our horn (power) like a wild ox and that we have been anointed with fresh oil. He is speaking of those who are planted in the house of the Lord (His presence). Verse 14 declares that they will be fat and flourishing. This is wonderful news for those who dwell in His presence, but the Lord has another purpose in it, outside of making sure His children exceed and excel. His agenda is for us to declare that He is upright and that He has no unrighteousness in Him. We, those who dwell with Him in the secret place of His presence, are God's advertisement.

How blessed we are to be able to spend time with Jesus! The Bible tells us in John 1:14 that the Word and the Spirit became flesh and dwelled among us. Jesus is the Word. He is the Light that guides us out of darkness (Ps. 119:105, 130) and into peace (Isa. 9:6–7; Luke 1:79). When we study the Word, allowing Jesus to abide in us (John 15:7), we can ask what we desire and it will be done. How can we be sure? Because we allow the very Master and keeper (Prince) of rest, safety, prosperity, health and favor (peace) to live and dwell in us. In other words, we let Jesus be Who He is on the inside of us. We can't help but have total victory in every situation and area of our lives. Have you ever wondered what eternal life is? The Bible states in John 17:3 that perpetual, forever, everlasting life (the Zoe life of God) is simply allowing God and His Son Jesus to have our lives and to understand that they are Who they say they are. It is receiving their truth and knowing for sure that it is just that—Truth. The closer we get to Him, the more deeply aware we are of His presence and the more we understand His ways. In a nutshell, the more we abide in His presence (the secret place), the more of His supernatural life we experience.

Rest is a position of absolute victory. When we take our place, hidden in Christ, and rest in the knowledge of who we are and *whose* we are, we are able to stand still and see the salvation of the Lord in every area of our lives (2 Chron. 20:17). His help is better than anything we could ever do for ourselves, so be diligent in entering into His rest and watch what He will do!

"You must learn to be still in the midst of activity and to be vibrantly alive in repose."

—Gandhi

Lord, I clearly see the need to abide in You, to rest in Your presence and acknowledge Your lordship in my life. I know that in doing so, it will cost me my self, but in return I will gain what I could never achieve alone—complete victory. I purpose to make abiding in Your rest my aim and focus, trusting that You have everything covered and as I stand still, I will see the Your triumphant plan for my life unfold!

Appendix

Prayer to initiate a life of rest in God

In order to experience true rest, we need to lay down our lives and yield ourselves to God. The first step in this process is salvation—making Jesus Christ Lord and Savior in your life. This is a free gift, available to all who come to Him and turn from sin to Him.

Scripture declares "For all have sinned and fall short of the glory of God" (Rom. 3:23). We are all guilty of sin, even if we are "good" people. "There is none righteous, no, not one" (Rom. 3:10). We are separated from God by our sin, but there is hope! God has invited each of us to become His children, adopted into his family. This occurs simply by renouncing our sin and receiving the lordship of Jesus Christ in our lives.

Scripture declares "If you confess with your mouth that Jesus is Lord and believe in your heart that God raised him from the dead, you will be saved. For it is by believing in your heart that you are made right with God, and it is by confessing with your mouth that you are saved" (Rom. 10:9-10 NLT). If you believe that Jesus died for you and are willing to give your life to Him, the rest is easy! To become a child of God, say this prayer from a sincere heart:

God in Heaven, I come to you and acknowledge that I am a sinner and need a savior. I believe that Jesus Christ, Your only begotten Son, came to pay the price for my sin on the cross. I believe He was crucified, died and was buried. I believe that He rose again on the third day and is seated at Your right hand. Today, I ask You to save me. Jesus, I confess You as my Lord and Savior. Come into my life and make me a child of God. I renounce sin and darkness and ask that You would flood my life with Your light. I declare that from this day forward, I will no longer live for myself, but for You. Help me to live my life for You and enter into the rest You have prepared for me, in Jesus' name. Amen.

Welcome to the family of God! You are His born-again child and He is so happy you made the decision to surrender your life to Him. You will never regret your decision.

References

Chapter 1

Helen H. Lemmel, "Turn Your Eyes Upon Jesus," 1922.

Chapter 2

Merriam-Webster. (2016). Merriam-Webster, Inc. (Version 3.4.3) [Mobile Application Software]. Retrieved from http://itunes.apple.com

Chapter 3

Merriam-Webster. (2016). Merriam-Webster, Inc. (Version 3.4.3) [Mobile Application Software]. Retrieved from http://itunes.apple.com

Chapter 4

Frangipane, Francis. *Holiness, Truth and the Presence of God.* Lake Mary: Charisma House, 2011.

Merriam-Webster. (2016). Merriam-Webster, Inc. (Version 3.4.3) [Mobile Application Software]. Retrieved from http://itunes.apple.com

Chapter 7
Merriam-Webster. (2016). Merriam-Webster, Inc. (Version 3.4.3) [Mobile Application Software]. Retrieved from http://itunes.apple.com

Chapter 9
Merriam-Webster. (2016). Merriam-Webster, Inc. (Version 3.4.3) [Mobile Application Software]. Retrieved from http://itunes.apple.com
Strong's Concordance. (2014). Orion Systems. (Version 3.0.2) [Mobile Application Software]. Retrieved from http://itunes.apple.com

All Chapters:
Scripture References
Hayford, Jack, W., editor. *New Spirit-Filled Life Bible.* Nashville: Thomas Nelson, Inc., 2002.
Tecarta. (2016). Tecarta, Inc. (Version 7.7) [Mobile Application Software]. Retrieved from http://itunes.apple.com.

Parenthetical Definitions
Strong's Concordance. (2014). Orion Systems. (Version 3.0.2) [Mobile Application Software]. Retrieved from http://itunes.apple.com.

References

Other Definitions

Merriam-Webster. (2016). Merriam-Webster, Inc. (Version 3.4.3) [Mobile Application Software]. Retrieved from http://itunes.apple.com.